Cardboard Citi

Written by Adrian Jackson

10 February – 10 March 2012

Performed at Riverside Studios
Crisp Road
London
W6 9RL

www.cardboardcitizens.org.uk

Approximate running time: 3 hours with one interval

Disclaimer: This is a work of fiction set against historical events. Any resemblance of characters to actual persons, living or dead, is purely coincidental.

LOTTERY FUNDED

A FEW MAN FRIDAYS

by Adrian Jackson

CREATIVE TEAM

Director	Adrian Jackson
Design	Fred Meller
Lighting	Natasha Chivers
Music & Soundtrack	David Baird
Video Design	SDNA
Movement & Choreography	Sarah Levinsky
Assistant Director	Cheryl Gallacher
Casting Director	Camilla Evans CDG
Community Participation Director	Tony McBride
Voice Coach	Tim Charrington
Composer's Assistant	Izzy Spint

CAST

Johanna Allitt	The Counsellor, Irene Fricke, Congressman Winn
Alasdair Craig	The Conservationist, Admiral Moorer, Jeffery Kitchen, Eric Sands, Congressman Lee Hamilton, John Todd
Sharon Duncan-Brewster	Madame Talate, Belinda Green, George T Churchill, Lynne Sands, Peter
Josian Fauzou	Pere Dussercle, the Teacher of Kreol, Marie Therese Mein, Benoit Renoir
Tom Hodgkins	Stu Barber, Bob Hope, M. Moulinie, Rolf Fricke, Commander Gary Sick,
Ansu Kabia	Prosper
Nicholas Khan	David Ottaway, Paul Nitze, E.H. Peck, S.S. Mandary, K. Young

Lecture attenders, airport queuers, internet nutters, community play participants and arisers from the dead, performed by:
Jamal Abubaker, Mohammed Arfan, Miguel Barros, Inderjit Batra, Ayomide Bodunrin, Kieran das Gupta, Edward Davies, Ester Escolano, Nick Fern, Chris Holland, Markus Junior, Vincent Moran, Kerry Norridge, Beatriz Pinto, Jamie Rivera Downey, Richard Rushton, Fi-fi Russell, Ben Smithies, Zviad Sokhadze, Shane Tanner, Melanie Vickers, Patricia Walsh, Yvonne Wickham.

Dancers from the Sega Chagos Archipelagos Rainbow Youth Club:
Jenny Edmond, Annabelle Florian, Anouchka Marisson, Hengride Permal, and Emilie Sagai.

PRODUCTION

Producer	Roy Luxford
Production Manager	Phil McCandlish
Company Stage Manager	Vicki Hambley
Deputy Stage Manager	Chiara Canal
Assistant Stage Manager	David Neill
Costume Supervisor	Heather Bagley
Press Agent	Sharon Kean, KeanLanyon
Marketing Consultant	Mark Slaughter
Photography	Simon Annand
Project Manager	Mike Sells
Assistant Producer	Stuart Grey
Marketing Manager	Petia Tzanova
Volunteer	Grace Perry

Film & Video credits:
Extract ABY 139. Film courtesy of the Imperial War Museum
Peaks of Limuria. Film courtesy of BFI National Archive/COI Crown copyright

Film and music credits correct at time of publication.

Thanks:
Thanks to Seewoo Sankar Mandary, Janette Esparon, XL Video, Interabang, Katy Rubin, Hugh McInally, Carrie Lukas, Emilia Teglia, Graeae Theatre Company, The People Show, Imperial War Museum, BFI, Public Records Office, Pinewood Studios, Conor Roche, Megan Hall, Wieden + Kennedy. Fred Meller is supported by Central Saint Martins College of Art and Design, The Centre for Performance, The University of the Arts London. Hengride Permal, Mylene Augustin and the Sega dancers, and the members and organisers of the Chagos Island Community Association (CICA). Everyone at Riverside Studios.

Set built and supplied by Q Division Leeds.

Adrian Jackson would like to thank:
Patrick Allen from the Ilfield Community College Choir, Richard Barber for kindly sharing letters and memories of his father, Marcus Booth, Roch Evenor, Philippa Gregory, Carolyn Murphy (Arts Development Manager). Those who participated in the play reading Chipo Chung, Neil Boorman, Dave Fishley, Kitty Martin, Simeon Moore, Clare Perkins and Trevor White.

ISLAND DREAMS

Robinson Crusoe

'the prototype of the British colonist…the whole Anglo-Saxon spirit is in Crusoe: the manly independence, the unconscious cruelty, the persistence, the slow yet efficient intelligence.'

James Joyce

Deleuze on Islands

Dreaming of islands – whether with joy or in fear, it doesn't matter – is dreaming of pulling away, of being already separate, far from any continent, of being lost and alone – or it is dreaming of starting from scratch, recreating, beginning anew…

Humans cannot live, nor live in security, unless they assume that the active struggle between earth and water is over, or at least contained. People like to call these two elements mother and father, assigning them gender roles according to the whim of their fancy. They must somehow persuade themselves that a struggle of this kind does not exist, or that it has somehow ended. In one way or another, the very existence of islands is the negation of this point of view, of this effort, this conviction. That England is populated will always come as a surprise; humans can live on an island only by forgetting what an island represents. Islands are either from before or for after humankind.

Gilles Deleuze, Desert Islands and Other texts, 1953-1974, trans. Michael Taormina, copyright 2004 Semiotext(e), 2002 Editions de Minuit, Paris.

Paranoia and reality

Roughly speaking, I think it's accurate to say that a corporate elite of managers and owners governs the economy and the political system as well, at least in very large measure. The people, so-called, do exercise an occasional choice among those who Marx once called "the rival factions and adventurers of the ruling class."

Noam Chomsky in a talk titled "Government in the Future" at the Poetry Center of the New York YM-YWHA, February 16, 1970 [2]

Under siege in April 2006, when a series of retired generals denounced him and called for his resignation in newspaper op-ed pieces, Donald Rumsfeld produced a memo after a conference call with military analysts. "Talk about Somalia, the Philippines, etc. Make the American people realize they are surrounded in the world by violent extremists," he wrote.

British Justice

I sought asylum in the UK rather than America because it is known as the one country that has laws that it follows.

Binyam Mohamed
(Ethiopian UK asylum-seeker interned in Guantánamo after extraordinary rendition flight)

Britain acknowledged today for the first time that US planes on "extraordinary rendition" flights stopped on British soil twice. The admission came from the foreign secretary, David Miliband, who apologised to MPs for incorrect information given by his predecessor, Jack Straw, and the former prime minister Tony Blair.

Miliband said the government had recently received information from Washington that two flights – one to Guantánamo Bay and one to Morocco – had stopped over at Diego Garcia, the British overseas territory in the Indian Ocean. Each plane carried a single terror suspect and neither of the men had been tortured, the CIA said.

"Contrary to earlier explicit assurances that Diego Garcia had not been used for rendition flights, recent US investigations have now revealed two occasions, both in 2002, when this had in fact occurred," Miliband told MPs. He said he had discussed the issue with the US Secretary of State, Condoleezza Rice.

"We both agree that the mistakes made in these two cases are not acceptable, and she shares my deep regret that this information has only just come to light," Miliband said.

Mark Tran, *The Guardian*, 21 February 2008:

Walter Benjamin's Angel of History

There is a painting by Klee called *Angelus Novus*. It shows an angel who seems about to move away from something he stares at. His eyes are wide, his mouth is open, his wings are spread. This is how the angel of history must look. His face is turned toward the past. Where a chain of events appears before *us, he* sees on single catastrophe, which keeps piling wreckage upon wreckage and hurls it at his feet. The angel would like to stay, awaken the dead, and make whole what has been smashed. But a storm is blowing from Paradise and has got caught in his wings; it is so strong that the angel can no longer close them. This storm drives him irresistibly into the future to which his back is turned, while the pile of debris before him grows toward the sky. What we call progress is this storm.

Walter Benjamin's 1940 work, "On the Concept of History," *Gesammelte Schriften* I, 691-704. Suhrkamp Verlag. Frankfurt am Main, 1974. Translation: Harry Zohn, from Walter Benjamin, *Selected Writings*, Vol. 4: 1938-1940 (Cambridge: Harvard University Press, 2003).

WRITER/DIRECTOR'S NOTE

I came across the story of the Chagossians in 2000, when I was lucky enough to deliver some training sponsored by the British Council in Mauritius, around Augusto Boal's *Theatre of the Oppressed*. This encounter also brought me into contact with the distinguished Mauritian theatre maker and activist, Henri Favory, who introduced me to Kreol as a language, and explained its significance. I saw the slums they lived in and was moved and horrified by the Chagos story, perhaps because the first instalments of it had occurred so recently, in fact during my teenage years under the Wilson government, only to be supported and repeated by successive governments right to the present day. I was amazed that I knew nothing about it, such a well-kept secret it was at the time. I have wanted to make a piece of theatre which could tell something of the story ever since.

The reactions it elicits amongst new listeners seem to fall broadly into two camps. Some, like me, are mortified that their governments could have been complicit, over such a long period, in the maltreatment of the Chagossian people. Others, and this has extended to elements of the media whom we have approached during the production process, have taken a rather harder attitude to it – much along the lines of the apocryphal *Times* headline, *Small Earthquake In Chile, Not Many Hurt* i.e. So what? It's only a couple of thousand people and the world's a tough place.

Unless of course you happen to have met some of those few thousand people, and then they start to acquire names and faces and humanity, and suddenly the earthquake's seismic waves stretch rather further. Mark Curtis has coined the term 'unpeople' to describe the phenomenon of the little people that governments routinely sweep aside in their quests for the various greater goods they are pursuing at the time. J.M. Coetzee has described Walter Benjamin's quest for 'a history centered on the sufferings of the vanquished, rather than on the achievements of the victors', as 'prophetic of the way in which history-writing has begun to think of itself in our lifetime.' What (hi)stories then do merit our attention, and what are the conditions which make them thus worthy of note? And what can we learn from these lesser-known episodes to help us understand the grand narratives of our time?

I have been working with marginalised and homeless people for some twenty years now. The Chagossian concept of *sagren* – something like the Brazilian *saudades* and the Russian *nostalgia* but with even more loss and pain – seemed to me to be something Cardboard Citizens participants could identify with; and indeed the various groups we work with have shown great empathy and engagement with this story of a whole nation evicted from its home.

Cardboard Citizens' history play cycle which began with *Mincemeat* – a WW2 epic about the post-mortem deployment of the body of a homeless man in an Allied deception operation – and continues with *A Few Man Fridays*, seeks to put 'unpeople' centre stage, with the dual aim of memorialising them and trying to understand what their treatment can teach us about the larger world. Both plays (a part three will come in two years' time, around the history of the Westminster gerrymandering scandal which took place late last century) are based largely on testimony and research, and the events they portray are substantially true.

I could not have made this play without the help of many people – in particular I want to thank Henri and Marie-France Favory, for their support and collaboration; David Vine and Laura Jeffery, for their support and serious scholarship which produced the key books on the Chagos story, which I commend to anyone interested in further study; Sarah Woods for her dramaturgical advice; Lottie Cantle, for her help during the research period; Richard Barber for kindly sharing letters and memories of his father; Seewoosankar Mandary for sharing his photographs; Janette Esparon for the photographs of her mother, Marie Therese Mein; Richard Gifford, for his help on the legal cases and his contacts; and all the Mauritians and Chagossians I interviewed in Mauritius and London, especially Olivier and Rita Bancoult, Mico Xavier, Cassam Uteem, Allen Vincatassan, Robin Mardemootoo. A very special thanks would have gone to Lisette Talate, with whom I conducted over six hours of interviews with – but sadly, she died on the second day of our rehearsals. So this production is dedicated to that great unsung freedom fighter, hunger striker and witness of the Chagossian struggle, Lisette Aurelie Talate (d. 4th January 2012, aged 70).

Adrian Jackson, January 2012

Johanna Allitt

The Counsellor, Irene Fricke, Congressman Winn

My grandma was one of the legendary landladies of Blackpool (where I was born) hence a love of fish and chips, camp lighting and the sea. I've performed in two recent productions for Cardboard Citizens: *Or Am I Alone?* (UK Tour/ Toynbee Studios), *Led Easy* (UK/ Austria Tour/Toynbee Studios). My other credits include *Cherry Pie* (film); *Scrub Up* (Queen Mary Studio/Live Art Development Agency); *For Sale, Death of a Salesman* (Yellow People's Theatre, Young Vic); *Cold Moon Rising* (Jermyn Street Theatre). I was a Space Vixen for many years in *Saucy Jack and the Space Vixens*, the musical. I also co-devised/produced the original Fringe First award-winning production (the Albany, Deptford; Assembly Rooms and the Pleasance, Edinburgh; Queen's Theatre, West End; The Nuffield Theatre, Southampton; Hackney Empire). I also love to sing and teach.

David Baird

Music and Soundtrack

I have been a supporter of & collaborator with Cardboard Citizens and director Adrian Jackson (and Terry O'Leary) right back to its beginnings, composing music/ soundtracks and musically directing shows including *The Lower Depths*, *Woyzeck*, *Mincemeat* (theatre and BBC radio), *Timon of Athens*, *Pericles*, *The Wall* and other projects... Of course I do a lot of other things away from Cardboard Citizens – I compose/ I direct / I write books / I'm a singer songwriter and I have travelled the world doing these things, but I always seem to find myself being lured back here- perhaps it's to do with synchronicity or perhaps it's because Adrian makes such damn good coffee!

Chiara Canal

Deputy Stage Manager

I worked for four years in Rome, Italy, as a Theatre Production Assistant but once arrived in London more than three years ago I moved to Stage Management.
Most recently I have worked at the Riverside Studios as a DSM for *Blind Date/27 Wagons Full of Cottons* (Make&Bake Productions). I also worked as a DSM for The Musical Theatre Academy, for Talawa Theatre Company (2011 tour of *KRUNCH* and *#I Am England* at the Lilian Baylis Studio at the Sadler's Wells) and at the Tricycle Theatre for *Judgment at Nuremberg*.
If I could bring just one thing to a desert island it would be Bob Dylan's album *Highway 61 Revisited*.

Natasha Chivers

Lighting Designer

I grew up in Yorkshire and moved to London twenty years ago where I fell in love with lighting things. I trained in technical theatre at LAMDA and went on to teach myself lighting design over the next twenty years. I live in London and like nothing more than a trip to seaside with friends or family in my campervan.

Alasdair Craig

The Conservationist, Admiral
Moorer, Jeffery Kitchen, Eric Sands,
Congressman Lee Hamilton,
Svangunjah, John Todd

After training at Webber Douglas
I spent several years touring the
world with the all male Shakespeare
Company, Propeller. Rehabilitation
back into the world of mixed sex
companies has followed, including:
Arcadia (Lowry Centre), *All My Sons*
(Leicester) and *The Quick* (Tristan
Bates Theatre) and on TV: *EastEnders*,
Doctors and *The Royal*.

Sharon Duncan-Brewster

Madame Talate, Belinda Green,
George T Churchill, Lynne Sands,
Peter

My first real experience of the acting
world was gifted to me at age of
six from The Anna Scher Children's
Theatre. My sincerest gratitude goes
out to Anna, without her I really
would not be here xxx. My most
recent TV performance was as Lisa,
in Channel Four's highly acclaimed
drama *Top Boy*. Last year I also
appeared in *Tiger Country* (Hampstead
Theatre), *The Swan* (National Theatre)
and *Yerma* (Gate Theatre). I LOVE
popcorn but let's not get into salt
or sweet, I don't want to get pigeon-
holed.

Josian Fauzou

Pere Dussercle, the Teacher of
Kreol, Marie Therese Mein, Benoit
Renoir

I joined the Henri Favory Theatre
Company in Mauritius in 1989, the
same year I qualified as a nurse.
After performing with the Company
for ten years, I worked with French
puppeteer Alexandra Shiva Melis
and performed with the Castaway
Community Theatre of Aberysthwyth.
I wrote and performed a one-man
show, *You Know What I Mean* at
the Aberystwyth Arts Centre in
2010. People often ask me 'Why
Aberystwyth?' It's because when
I look at the sea, I know that
somewhere over the horizon is my
homeland 'akot mo lonbri antere'
('where my umbilical cord is buried')
– an old Kreol saying – and I feel
close to it.

SDNA
Video Design

SDNA is a creative studio based in
London producing distinctive digital
artwork.
We are dedicated to explore
techniques of interaction within
public spaces, using emerging
technologies and blurring the
boundaries of creative disciplines.
Our interdisciplinary approach,
integrating site-responsive installation
and live performance, aims to widen
the scope of digital art. Over the
last seven years we have developed
and presented digital artwork and
theatrical productions for museums,
fashion labels, city councils, musicians
and many more. Our work varies
from audio visual installation and
performance to interactive public art.
Regularly working throughout Europe,
previous international projects have
taken us as far as Russia and French
Polynesia. In London venues have
included the Victoria and Albert
Museum, the ICA, The Roundhouse
and the Whitechapel Gallery.

Cheryl Gallacher
Assistant Director

I first encountered the work of Cardboard Citizens whilst studying English Literature/Writing and Performance at the University of York. Since then, I have most recently directed *Chapel Street*, which was performed at the Old Red Lion and the Liverpool Everyman and Playhouse (2011) – the same year I was selected for the Young Vic Springboard Project for emerging directors. If I could take one thing to a desert island, it would have to be my dog Paddy.

Vicki Hambley
Company Stage Manager

I have been working with Cardboard Citizens on various projects over the last 5 years. These plays include *Three Blind Mice*, *Or Am I Alone*, *Up on the Roof*, *An Open Book* and *Mincemeat*. I also work regularly with Half Moon Young People's Theatre, Theatre Venture and Face Front Inclusive Theatre. I moved to the UK in 2007, love travelling and playing sports. I hate restrictions on my travel and watching sports.

Tom Hodgkins
Stu Barber, Bob Hope, M. Moulinie, Rolf Fricke, Commander Gary Sick

Having come into acting from a Masters Degree in Industrial Robotics, my career in theatre has ranged for a long stint at the RSC including *The Histories* to the National Theatre and Broadway with *Guys and Dolls* and *Not About Nightingales* by Tennessee Williams via the David Glass Ensemble (*Mosquito Coast*) and Headlong (*Decade*). I also narrate documentaries and audio books, not to mention the odd film (the last was *Hanna* – dir Jon Wright) and TV (the last was *Hustle*).

Adrian Jackson
Writer and Director

I started Cardboard Citizens in 1991, and it rather dominates my life. I have directed numerous Forum Theatre shows, a *Lower Depths* and a *Beggar's Opera*, and enjoyed a fruitful relationship with the RSC, directing co-productions of *Pericles* and *Timon of Athens*. A couple of years ago we successfully revived *Mincemeat*, one of many site-specific pieces Cardboard Citizens has made. I am fortunate enough to travel a lot, usually teaching Theatre of the Oppressed, which is how I came upon this story. To relax, I cook or cycle – not at the same time.

Ansu Kabia
Prosper

I've been acting in the business for over six years now having spent time at drama school despite the fact that I did Maths and Physics at A-level. I've appeared in numerous plays in a number of theatres including The Library Theatre Manchester, the Arcola Theatre, Upstairs at the Gatehouse and Harlow Playhouse. I have worked with the NITRO theatre company and I recently completed three years with the RSC. Outside of all that I absolutely love to cycle.

Nicholas Khan

David Ottaway, Paul Nitze, E.H. Peck, S.S. Mandary, K. Young

I enjoy collaborating, those I have sweated with include; The London Bubble, The Royal Exchange, RSC, Steven Berkoff, Shared Experience, Soho Theatre, Shakespeare's Globe and recently The Liverpool Playhouse. On TV amongst others *Trial and Retribution, Spooks, Getting Out Alive!, The Fades* and *Outnumbered*, and on Radio the prize winning *Letters from Guantanamo*. I am happy to return to the Citz in a cherry picked narrative unravelling some more delightful home truths. Throughout the day I freefall – a passenger to the whims of Gene and Pina.

Sarah Levinsky

Movement & Choreography

Working as Associate Director at Cardboard Citizens I explored dance with asylum seekers and discovered I was a choreographer. In a fluctuating space between dance and theatre, work includes Co-Directorship of Mapping4D, commissions for Theatre Royal Plymouth, Chisenhale Dance Space, and currently, development of *Plastic Island*, a dance on carrier bags, as a Supported Artist at The Hat Factory.

Phil McCandlish

Production Manager

I have worked in the industry for over 25 years during which time I have worked with some lovely people and some not so lovely (they know who they are). When I am not working around the world I live by the seaside with my wife and two children.

Fred Meller

Designer

I am an established Theatre Designer and Scenographer, and first worked with Cardboard Citizens 16 years ago. Since then I have also designed, amongst others, for The Almeida, The Watermill, The Gate, The RNT Studio, and Grid Iron. I have exhibited and won awards in the UK and internationally and our work with Cardboard Citizens is part of the V&A's permanent Theatre collection. I became a Fellow of The Arts Foundation, and I teach at The University of the Arts CSM, and I am an Executive Director of the Society of British Theatre Designers

David Neill

Assistant Stage Manager

I got into Theatre aged eight when I joined Hazlitt Youth Theatre where I performed in many musicals and plays until I had to leave to go to drama school at 18. I went to college to learn Technical theatre for two years and fell in love with Stage Management. I have recently just finished a run of *The Railway Children* as ASM. I now have four fish named Richard, Hyacinth, Tarquin and Cathy.

cardboard
citizens

Cardboard Citizens has been changing the lives of homeless and displaced people through theatre and the performing arts for over 20 years.

Recent productions include *Mincemeat* (Evening Standard award) by Adrian Jackson and Farhanna Sheikh, *Three Blind Mice* by Bola Agbaje, *Or Am I Alone?* by Lizzie Nunnery, *Led Easy* by David Watson, *Woyzeck*, and with the Royal Shakespeare Company – *Timon of Athens*, *Pericles* and *Visible* by Sarah Woods.

All productions feed into and are supported by Cardboard Citizens' Hostel Tour and Workshop Programme (for people with experience of homelessness) and ACT NOW (specifically for young people not in employment, education or training). Performances and workshops are delivered all year round, where participants can work towards accredited qualifications. They can also access tailored one-to-one support from trained advice and guidance workers.

Wherever possible, the company employs ex-homeless people. In addition, 10% of our tickets are given away each year to people who have experience of homelessness or social exclusion.

If you would like to become a friend of the company by donating as little as £3 per month, please visit www.cardboardcitizens.org.uk

Friends receive up to date information about the work of Cardboard Citizens, plus priority invitations to future public performances and events.

Cardboard Citizens
26 Hanbury Street
London
E1 6QR
Tel: 020 7247 7747
Email: mail@cardboardcitizens.org.uk
Web: www.cardboardcitizens.org.uk

Twitter: @CardboardCitz and #FewManFridays
Facebook: Cardboard Citizens
You Tube: CardboardCitzTv

Registered Charity Number: 1042457

Cardboard Citizens Staff

To email our staff send a message to firstname@cardboardcitizens.org.uk

Adrian Jackson – Artistic Director and Chief Executive
Cathy Weatherald – Project Manager
Kathrine Quiller-Croasdell – Programme Director
Lisa Caughey – Deputy Chief Executive
Mike Sells – Project Manager
Petia Tzanova – Marketing Manager
Stuart Grey – Administrator/ Assistant Producer
Tasneem Afsaruddin – IAG Worker
Terry O'Leary – Associate Artist
Tony McBride – Director of Projects
Yago De La Torre – Database Administrator
Zahid Tabbassum – Finance Manager

BOARD MEMBERS

Andy W Ganf
Barbra Mazur
Graham Fisher – Chair
John Moffatt – Treasurer
Jonathan Sandall
Mary Ann Hushlak
Mojisola Adebayo
Philip Parr
Sean Dalton
Sian Edwardes-Evans
Simon Hughes
Sue Timothy

Cardboard Citizens Theatre of the Oppressed Training

Cardboard Citizens is one of the UK's leading practitioners of Forum Theatre, offering specialist training courses in all aspects of the Theatre of the Oppressed.

These courses are led by Adrian Jackson, Augusto Boal's translator and frequent collaborator, with the participation of members of Cardboard Citizens, the UK's only homeless people's professional theatre company. The courses, all held in London, offer an ensemble of techniques and approaches and are suitable for anyone interested in using theatre to encourage social change.

For further information or to book please visit www.cardboardcitizens.org.uk or contact mail@cardboardcitizens.org.uk

Support for *A Few Man Fridays*

Cardboard Citizens would like to thank the following funders for their support of *A Few Man Fridays*:

Arts Council England – Grants for the Arts
British Council
Esmée Fairbairn Foundation
Evan Cornish Foundation
Mind Unit
Paul Hamlyn Foundation
The Mercers' Company

Supporting Cardboard Citizens' work

Very special thanks to Cardboard Citizens' Ambassador, Kate Winslet, and all the other individuals and friends whose ongoing support makes our work possible.

Cardboard Citizens would also like to thank the following organisations and businesses for their support in the financial year 2011/12:

Allen & Overy Foundation
Arts Council England
Ashridge Business School
BBC Performing Arts Fund
Big Lottery Fund
British Council
Buzzacott Stuart Defries Memorial Fund
Capital International Limited
City of Westminster Charitable Trust
D'Oyly Carte Charitable Trust
Ecorys
Environmental Mobile Control Ltd
Esmée Fairbairn Foundation
Exemplas
Give a Car Ltd
Guildford Academics Associates
Harold Hyam Wingate Foundation
Hon M L Astor 1969 Charitable Trust
J Paul Getty Jr Charitable Trust
Linda Meyers LLP
Lombard Street Research
London Borough of Hackney
London Borough of Tower Hamlets
London Chamber of Commerce and Industry
London Councils
Lord Faringdon Charitable Trust
McPin Foundation
Mission Fish UK
N Smith Charitable Settlement
National Lottery through the Olympic Lottery Distributor managed by East London Business Alliance
Paul Hamlyn Foundation
Peter Minet Trust
Pret Foundation Trust
Religious Society of Friends
Reuben Brothers Charitable Trust
Royal Borough of Kensington & Chelsea
Schroeder Forbes Ltd
Souter Charitable Trust
The Allen and Overy Foundation
The Charles S French Charitable Trust
The Coutts Charitable Trust
The De Laszlo Foundation
The Drapers' Company
The Ernest Hecht Foundation
The Henry Smith Charity
The Joan Strutt Charitable Trust
The New Court Charitable Trust
The Odin Charitable Trust
The Rind Foundation
The Sir Jules Thorn Charitable Trust
The Syder Foundation
The William and Christine Eynon Charity
Trust for London
Wieden + Kennedy

ADRIAN JACKSON

A FEW MAN FRIDAYS

OBERON BOOKS
LONDON

WWW.OBERONBOOKS.COM

First published in 2012 by Oberon Books Ltd
521 Caledonian Road, London N7 9RH
Tel: +44 (0) 20 7607 3637 / Fax: +44 (0) 20 7607 3629
e-mail: info@oberonbooks.com
www.oberonbooks.com

A catalogue record for this book is available from the British Library.

ISBN: 978-1-84943-218-4

Cover design by interabang.uk.com

Printed and bound by CPI Group (UK) Ltd, Croydon, CR0 4YY.

I sought asylum in the UK rather than America because it is known as the one country that has laws that it follows.

Binyam Mohamed (Ethiopian UK Asylum-seeker interned in Guantánamo after extraordinary rendition flight)

Notes

This script contains references to videos, some of which are on the internet, some in the Imperial War Museum, some research interviews held by CCs; internet links are liable to change, and may require some searching to recover. These should be viewed alongside the script whenever possible.

/ signifies interruption or overlap.

A Few Man Fridays produced by Cardboard Citizens premiered on 15th February 2012, at Riverside Studios, London with the following cast:

Johanna Allitt	Mary, a Counsellor,
	Irene Fricke, a Yachtswoman
	Congressman Winn, an American
Alasdair Craig	Teddy Hibbert, a Conservationist,
	Admiral Moorer,
	Jeffery Kitchen, a US diplomat
	Eric Sands, a Yachtsman
	Congressman Lee Hamilton,
	Chair of a House Sub-Committee
Sharon Duncan-Brewster	Madame Lisette Talate, a Chagossian
	Belinda Green, Miss World 1971
	George T Churchill,
	a Country Director at State Department
	Lynne Sands, a Yachtswoman
	Peter, a New Labour Politician
Josian Fauzou	Pere Dussercle, a Roman Catholic Priest
	The Teacher of Kreol, a Chagossian
	Marie Therese Mein, a Chagossian
	Benoit Renoir, a Sailor
Tom Hodgkins	Stu Barber, a Naval Planner
	Bob Hope,
	M. Moulinie, a Plantation Manager
	Rolf Fricke, a Yachtsman
	Commander Gary Sick,
	a Director at International Security, State Dept
Ansu Kabia	Prosper, a Man
Nicholas Khan	David Ottaway, a Washington Post Journalist
	Paul Nitze, Assistant Secretary of Defence
	E.H. Peck, a Civil Servant in the Foreign Office
	S.S. Mandary, a Meteorologist
	K. Young, a Broadcaster

All other parts performed by the company.

Director	Adrian Jackson
Design	Fred Meller
Lighting	Natasha Chivers
Music & Soundtrack	David Baird
Video Design	SDNA
Movement & Choreography	Sarah Levinsky
Assistant Director	Cheryl Gallacher

PREFACE

PROSPER is sitting with a dog. Blackout. Lightning. FATHER DUSSERCLE prays.

DUSS: O seigneur de toute creation – N'est pas un rêve que je viens de vivre?

Sweep of lighthouse light onto audience.

DUSS: I feel I have awoken from a dream!

At last, cutting through the dark screen of our too too long night comes the lighthouse beam of our beloved Île Maurice, the light of deliverance, after the hours of tragedy on that fateful night 20th June 1935.

I, Roger Dussercle, shepherd of your flock scattered across thousands of miles of the Indian Ocean, give thanks, both for myself and for my parish, from Agalega to Salomon, from Peros Banhos to Diego Garcia, from Île Aigle to Île Danger…

For ten years now, I have made my annual pilgrimage to minister to my congregation on les Îles Chagos by the good ship Diego. There are dreamers who try to imagine what an island of Happiness could be – if they could see these islands they would surely fix upon them – des émeraudes parfaites sur une mer azurée.

This time we approached Eagle Island with our cargo of 30 passengers, the sea was calm and tranquil, les brisants à fleur d'eau entourent des petites crêtes neigeuses et bouillonnantes. We dropped anchor, to load up copra and oil of coco.

At two o'clock that day, without warning, the wind changed to north west – the boat swung round presenting its stern to the reefs. The captain immediately dropped a second anchor.

But the wind redoubles her violence, the breakers push us harder towards the land. I gather all the passengers – and we say the rosary *(He prays.)* Je vous salue, Marie, pleine de grâce. Le Seigneur est avec vous. Vous êtes bénie entre toutes les femmes.

The good ship Diego starts dragging on its anchors, heads of coral are emerging from the deep, the coconut palms of the shore grow larger and closer, too close. *(Prayer continues.)* Et Jésus, le fruit de vos entrailles, est béni. Sainte Marie, Mère de Dieu, Priez pour nous, pauvres pécheurs, maintenant et à l'heure de notre mort. Amen.

Only one thing for it – throw forth the sheet anchor, *l'ancre de misèricorde*, the heaviest on board. Hold Faites que ça tienne faites que ça tienne faites que ça tienne… It bites the seafloor, the cable stretches, the boat ceases its backward movement. Merci seigneur. For a moment the boat is still. But suddenly the sheet anchor cable snaps, and ricochets down the deck like a wounded snake, its burden dumped on the deep.

The sea, the wind, the night, all come down upon us to conjure our fate, as if the demons of the ocean had come together for the hellish Sabbath. I take refuge with the passengers below decks, Ave Maria full of grace…

A terrible crash shakes the vessel – the main mast has gone – the ship is breaking from within. Three lifeboats are swept away, dancing like corks on the water.

Distress flares are launched, a cannon shot tears through night. Torches on the shoreline, the coconut palms are arms waving to us, one man is pushing out a boat, a pirogue, at this point he is a man without a name, but he represents salvation…if only he can reach us, if only he can reach us, if only we may get to know his name, if only… que Dieu lui vienne en aide.

Noise of storm bleeds into noise of applause, for the lecture of Teddy Hibbert, CONSERVATIONIST.

SCENE 1
Caption: Queen Mary University, London, July 2010

This scene is a filleted version of the first half of the final scene of the play. A short series of extracts of that scene is performed, with blackouts and compression sounds in between. They concern mainly a white man, the CONSERVATIONIST, who is just finishing a lecture, and a black man, PROSPER, who engages in conversation with him.

CONSERV: We did it. The dream has come true. Yeah! *(He ends in fist in air gesture.)*

Blackout.

He is speaking intently into the microphone.

When I first found the giant manta, this noble creature had nowhere to run. Like an aeroplane running out of fuel –

and those of you who have seen it know that it is a bit like a small aeroplane, up to seven metres from wing to wing, sleek, black, double hulled, beautiful.

Blackout.

He meets PROSPER.

CONSERV: Hello.

PROSPER: You don't remember me?

CONSERV: I have a face recognition defect, face-blindness, I don't recognise people, sometimes I take photos.

PROSPER: Like a spy.

CONSERV: Most people have a kind of rolodex of faces in their head, to recognise others, I have to take photos.

PROSPER: You never took a photograph of me.

Blackout.

CONSERV: Look you seem to be angry with me – I don't know why – we don't even know each other.

PROSPER: I am not a significant other.

Blackout.

CONSERV: That's not what I said, and not what I think.

Of course you are more important than a turtle.

Blackout.

He is on his mobile.

Okay. So when exactly did Ronnie Barker go missing?

Blackout.

PROSPER is looking at the screen of the CONSERVATIONIST's laptop.

PROSPER: *(Referring to the projected images.)* Who're all the people?

CONSERV: Friends, acquaintances, I told you I suffer from faceblindness, it's none of your business.

That's my son,

PROSPER: You need a photo to remember what your son looks like?

CONSERV: *(Snatching back his laptop.)* Of course not, that's my screen saver.

Blackout.

PROSPER: Listen? Do you hear?

There is nothing.

CONSERV: What?

Hear what?

We hear a bell, the CONSERVATIONIST doesn't.

PROSPER: That's what you call a wake-up call. We call it the bellcall.

Blackout.

A dog ball bounces on from stage right – the COUNSELLOR picks it up.

Blackout.

SCENE 2

A lighthouse sweep may dazzle us, a collage of voices and faces, different parts of the stage, different scales, probably a bit mad, overlapping. A sliding projection screen crosses from left to right. First MADAME TALATE, on screen in Kreol – consistent image, in movement – brief extract of her. Flick through images, stop at real photo of STU BARBER – actor, live beside him, speaks off.

STU: Ever since I was a kid I dreamt of desert islands. I was a sickly kinda kid, stayed home too much, used to collect stamps from islands – never imagined it would end up this way.

Bob Hope on screen, still image, recorded sound, fragment of Xmas show. Flick through various Americans, Paul Nitze, E.H. Peck, Mrs Thatcher, her image, her voice, Mickey Mouse sound, still images, Seewoosagur Ramgoolam, Robin Cook, Pere Dussercle, images of some of the actual actors, dancing around between these fragments, back and forth, till finally settling on image of STU BARBER. We see old-ish actor standing next to picture of STU, then being interviewed by a Washington Post *JOURNALIST, David Ottaway.*

STU: I guess I would have been about 12.

JOURNO: If you don't mind my asking/ [when would that have been]

STU: 1928 maybe – we were living in New Rochelle.

JOURNO: Just outsida New York.

STU: Days I was sick, I stayed home, arranging my stamps.

JOURNO: You were an avid stamp collector.

STU: It was stamps or a dog, and my folks wouldn't have a dog in the house, so they kept me quiet with stamps.

JOURNO: Less trouble than a dog.

STU: I should say so. Anyway, sometimes I would be baby-sitting this kid Tommy from next door, or maybe he was supposed to be looking out for me, he was a pain in the ass.

JOURNO: How so?

STU: He would sit there, playing yo-yo, asking questions like you are now, 'cept he wasn't from the *Washington Post*, this was just him jabbering, like: What are you doing Stu?

JOURNO: What are you doing Stu?

STU: And I would say, putting my stamps in order, what does it look like, and he would say –

JOURNO: Order of what?

STU: That's right, and I would say, order of favouriteness.

JOURNO: Where are they from Stu? *(JOURNALIST actor takes up the role of TOMMY.)*

Caption: New Rochelle, 1928.

STU is arranging stamps, cross-checking with atlas; we see this through camera focussed on table. STU guards his activity, avoiding being spied on.

STU: Isn't your Ma supposed to have picked you up by now?

TOMMY: She works late Thursdays.

STU: I get them from Bernstein's mainly – sometimes my Dad brings them when I get sick –

TOMMY: I mean where are they from, which countries have you got?

STU: They're islands. I only collect islands. Especially desert islands.

TOMMY: Why?

STU: I just like them.

TOMMY: Which one is your most favourite then?

STU: Give me another go with that thing and I'll show you.

TOMMY: OK. *(STU takes yo-yo.)*

STU: Most favourite right now is… *(Gives him stamp.)* The Falkland Islands – which is just there.

Pointing on the map.

We see a projection of stamp and map.

TOMMY: Is he like the King of the Falkland Islands?

STU: He's the English King – the Falkland Islands belongs to England, which is there…

TOMMY: How come it belongs to them – it's like a million miles away?

STU: That's just how it is.

TOMMY: That penguin looks like it's gonna eat that fish.

STU: It's a whale, not a fish –

TOMMY: Has the Falkland Island got a desert?

STU: A what? – Desert island means it's deserted, it's nothing to do with sand.

TOMMY: Are the Falkland Islands deserted?

STU: I dunno – there's obviously penguins ther…

TOMMY: Robinson Crusoe is on a desert island.

STU: Wrong, he thinks its deserted but A.) there's a dog, and B.) there's natives there. Have you read it?

TOMMY: No.

STU: There's his Man Friday.

TOMMY: His man who?

STU: His faithful servant – he's a native. Never mind. Reckon I wouldn't mind having myself my own island.

TOMMY: Why?

STU: Cos then I wouldn't have to answer dumb questions, that's why.

STU cannot make the yo-yo work.

TOMMY: I could be your Man Friday.

STU: Yeah, sure/ This thing's stupid.

TOMMY: I don't reckon a person can own an island.

STU: A person can own anything, it's just a matter of buying it. Betcha Howard Hughes could own an island, and he could fly one of his planes there and land on the water, any time he wanted.

TOMMY: Wow –

STU: Cos he doesn't like people, and he likes to be secret, and if you're on an island no one knows what you're doing.

TOMMY: What about the people on the island?

STU: There wouldn't be people on the island, would there. He would choose an island where there weren't any people, that's the whole point.

TOMMY: What if there were cannibals?

STU: Cannibals aren't real.
Here's your dodo back. *(Returns yo-yo.)*

TOMMY: Yo-yo.

STU: I call it a dodo

TOMMY: Tarzan's <u>always</u> fighting cannibals.

STU: Tarzan isn't real, cannibals aren't real. Who would want to eat people? Now scoot.

TOMMY: *(Making way.)* They might be bad people. What if there was nothing else to eat.

STU: Anyway, there won't be people on the island, it doesn't work if there are people there.

TOMMY: So it's a desert island.

STU: OK, it's a desert island, with no people, no Tarzan, no cannibals. Now why don't you read the funnies if you're fed up with your dodo?

TOMMY: Yo-yo.

STU: If you say so. *(Reverting to now.)* – Yeah, it was kinda like that, believe it or not, it's all true.

On the projection, the penguin dives from the stamp into the sea of the map.

On the sliding projection screen, we watch a brief extract of Mickey's Man Friday, from the late 1920s
http://www.youtube.com/watch?v=VqRtMgOZuPA

SCENE 3A
Caption: London, late 2011

COUNSELLOR: *(She is speaking into recording device.)* – He started coming to see me in Summer six years ago. Called himself Prosper, don't have a second name. He was one of my first – It was hot. I was raw.

Caption: London, May 2005

PROSPER is there. She wrestles with box, cards go flying.

She is picking them up.

PROSPER: I hear voices, *(Correction.)* I have heard voices, powerful voices.

COUNS: OK.

PROSPER: I smoked a lot of ganga.

COUNS: Right.

PROSPER: They say there's a connection.

COUNS: Not proven, but strong circumstantial evidence.

PROSPER: Guilty as charged.

COUNS: What do the voices say?

PROSPER: The voice I hear most is the one I understand least. Like she's speaking in tongues.

COUNS: Do you only hear the voice or do you see a person?

PROSPER: Both –

COUNS: And this is a woman.

PROSPER: An old lady, well old. Like an African lady, but I don't think she's speaking an African language.

COUNS: Who do you think she might be?

PROSPER: I don't know her.

COUNS: Some people who hear voices find it useful to speak to them –

PROSPER: Mad people maybe. I don't wanna be one of them mumbling people in the street.

COUNS: Tell me a bit about yourself.

PROSPER: Grew up in a Rasta commune in Stockwell.

COUNS: Your parents were practising Rastafarians –

PROSPER: Don't know my parents, turns out my Mum left me there when I was eight and went back to Mauritius or maybe the Seychelles. I lived in the squat with the Rastas till *(Acting Rasta.)* the Babylon came down 'pon us with a vengeance –

COUNS: Babylon –

PROSPER: The police raided the place and evicted all the brothers and sisters and closed it down.

COUNS: That sounds traumatic.

PROSPER: It was mad. They was peaceful people, doing no harm. Just smoking a bit of weed and t'ing. Didn't deserve to be thrown out like that.

COUNS: You say it 'turned out' your Mum left you in the commune and went back to Mauritius – when did you discover this?

PROSPER: Few months back. I met one of the elders in Brixton. He told me. Anyway she wasn't my real mum – I just call her my Mum.

COUNS: Why do you say that?

PROSPER: She was white, think she was British, I don't know – she must have been living out there.

COUNS: In Mauritius?

PROSPER: She was a hippy, fell in love with a Rastaman.

COUNS: Your Dad.

PROSPER: Maybe – not sure.

COUNS: So you are Mauritian?

PROSPER: The brother said my roots were in Diego Garcia, that's all he knew.

COUNS: Now I am getting confused too. Is that in Mexico?

PROSPER: It's an island – part of the Chagos Islands – nobody knows it –

COUNS: Sorry.

PROSPER: I didn't know about it either, just looked it up on a map.

COUNS: Have you ever been back there? Would you like to go back there?

PROSPER: I got no papers, no passport. Officially stateless.

COUNS: What about your real mother?

PROSPER: Don't even know her name. She could be dead. That's what I feel.

COUNS: You feel grief.

PROSPER: Every day. Feel a sadness bigger than my heart. Feel lost. *(He is on the edge of tears – gathers himself.)*

COUNS: Prosper. There's nothing wrong with feeling grief. Have you spoken to anyone about this before?

PROSPER: I tried to smoke it out of me, stopped that now.

COUNS: Do you find your emotions are closer to the surface?

PROSPER: I get angry easy, I cry easy, sometimes think I am going crazy, what can you do.

COUNS: Well, if you're asking, I can listen. I can ask questions.

PROSPER: I got questions, it's answers I need. 'Bout me.

COUNS: You have gaps in your history, talking to someone may fill in some of those gaps.

PROSPER: My history.

COUNS: How you have become who you are.

PROSPER: History.

COUNS: Knowing our past can help us understand the present better.

PROSPER: I got no memory, too much ganga.

COUNS: You locked down memory as a way of coping with grief. Speak to relations, look at family photos, they might jog your memory –

PROSPER: Thought you were supposed to listen. I am on my own. Got no relations. One man band.

COUNS: Then we can try to find other ways to recover your history. The internet is amazing, it's amazing what you find there.

PROSPER: The internet is a trap, it watches you back, it's all recorded, I used to look at it all the time.

COUNS: Talk to people from the commune maybe, see if you can do some research on your island in the library... Where do you live now?

PROSPER: Housing Association – now they're evicting me too. They're taking me to court for arrears.

COUNS: Citizens Advice could help you with that.

PROSPER: When I stopped with the weed, I started having dreams.

COUNS: What happens?

PROSPER: I see the same faces over and over, different places, different outfits, same people. It's weird.

COUNS: It's not so weird – What do you dream about?

PROSPER: Lots of things. Islands. Airplanes. Dogs, all sorts of weirdness – donkeys wearing blindfolds.

COUNS: The dreams disturb you.

PROSPER: Not always. Sometimes I wake up feeling happy, till I remember it was only a dream.

COUNS: Tell me a happy dream.

Beat.

PROSPER: I only have fragments.

COUNS: Give me a fragment.

PROSPER: Everyone is dancing, round a fire.

COUNS: Who is everyone?

PROSPER: Children, adults, everyone. Big fire. Lots of people.

Sound, video, black and white Sega, very powerful, one minute.

COUNS: Is this a memory of the commune?

PROSPER: Could be.

SCENE 3B

While the dream image plays, the CONSERVATIONIST is on his way somewhere when his mobile rings.

CONSERV: Hello – this is he.

Yes – hi, thank you, I got the email, I was going to call you, just trying to work out a good time with the time difference.

Well I have to run it past my wife, but in principle, yes, I would be delighted to attend.

Okay, yes, that's right, I was in the city for a while, came back to marine biology a few years back, after I had the giant manta moment.

Yes, I find myself more and more drawn in the conservation direction.

Great. Count me in – Of course, home of the dodo, I get it. Without wishing to be indelicate, is the foundation paying for all this, flights, hotel the lot?

Wonderful, I have no problem with their agenda at all, I just wanted to know. It's good to know that there are people in the States who care.

I'll send you an email, greatly looking forward.

SCENE 3C

Back to the counselling session.

COUNS: What else?

PROSPER: Dogs, I dream of dogs. All kinds of dogs.

COUNS: What are the dogs doing?

PROSPER: Running about and catching fish.

COUNS: In the sea.

PROSPER: But I can't swim –

COUNS: In your dream –

PROSPER: No, I can't swim in life.

COUNS: Sorry.

PROSPER: And then soldiers come chasing us and we run like crazy – it's like a horror movie.

COUNS: Where are you?

PROSPER: I am running with the dogs.

COUNS: Do you think the dogs represent something? What comes to mind?

PROSPER: Represent?

COUNS: In dreams things aren't always what they seem. What do you think the dogs the soldiers are hunting stand for?

PROSPER: Dogs. They represent dogs. They stand for dogs. Why do they to have to represent something?

COUNS: They don't, necessarily – Tell me about the planes.

PROSPER: Planes that can land on water, flying boat-type planes, and bombers, big motherfucker bombers –

COUNS: And what else?

PROSPER: That's it.

COUNS: Do you have a dog?

PROSPER: Not right now. I'm on my own.

COUNS: *(Beat.)* I am afraid our time is up.

PROSPER: – Is that it?

PROSPER leaves. It may be that he crosses, on exit, with STU BARBER waiting for the next scene, and looks at him, like he has seen him before. PROSPER may pass through any other scene.

COUNS: *(To recording device.)* I didn't read the notes from the referring psychiatrist till later he had been stabilised on a regime of minor anti-psychotics after some kind of episode. Some behaviour might have indicated paranoia – the business about same faces different places... But then... they <u>were</u> out to get him...

We may see some dream, including the donkey from the Imperial War Museum film of the Chagos Islands.

SCENE 4

Caption: The Pentagon, Arlington Virginia, April 1961

Throughout the play there is a convention that when actors are playing real historical figures, we see projected the flicking-through of a rolodex of photos, till it lands on an actual photo(s) of the relevant character – the actor may stand alongside the image for a moment, before moving into the scene.

April 1961. ADMIRAL MOORER is waiting to brief Assistant Secretary of Defence PAUL NITZE who is engaged in keep-fit routine. STU BARBER waits outside, he plays with a yo-yo.

MOORER: Secretary Nitze, Sir.

NITZE: Come in Moorer.

MOORER: Admiral Rivero told me you wanted a full briefing on the strategic island concept.

NITZE: Burke and Rivero have kept me in the loop, but I am keen to hear it from the horse's mouth, so to speak. If I am to persuade the President, I will need all the ammunition available.

MOORER: Mr Secretary, I have brought the horse, in person/ as it were.

NITZE: The horse?

MOORER: Stu Barber Sir. He has been chomping at the bit since way back when. It's his baby.

NITZE: The civilian guy – heard a lot about him. Wheel him in.

MOORER: Stu?

STUART BARBER stops yo-yoing, enters.

MOORER: Assistant Secretary Nitze, Stu Barber.

STU: Pleased to meet you Sir.

NITZE: How long have you been working on this Barber?

STU: More than five years Sir, we started Op 93 in 1955.

NITZE: You're not a soldier Barber.

STU: I was stationed in Hawaii during the war Sir, never saw active service, no Sir, not for want of trying.

MOORER: Our Stu is one of those perennial backroom boys, Mr Secretary, always dreaming things up.

NITZE: We need dreamers Barber, without dreamers there would be no America. Tell me about your islands dream, Sir, and tell it good, because what you tell me I will be telling Mr Kennedy and our future may depend upon it.

STU: Op 93 was tasked with looking into the future Sir, scenario planning –

MOORER: 10-15 years down the line, with regard to the relative power position of the Soviet bloc versus the free world.

STU: Within the next five to ten years, we assume that virtually all of Africa, and certain Middle Eastern and Far Eastern countries presently under Western control will gain either complete independence or a high degree of autonomy.

MOORER: Sure as eggs is eggs.

STU: One product of this trend will be the withdrawal, denial or restriction of Western military base facilities in many of these areas.

NITZE: So your 'concept' involves the development of a 'hedge' against these eventualities.

MOORER: The Brits have already expressed their intention to withdraw from Aden, which would significantly weaken our position in the Indian Ocean.

STU: And the Soviets have displayed an active interest in the area.

MOORER: We're pretty sure they're already making mischief in Somalia –

NITZE: I read the intercepts, I know the nightmare – half the world ends up wearing grey suits, with Mr Kruschev's ugly mug on every wall – it's the dream I want, the dream – what's your plan Barber?

STU: Get hold of a bunch of islands now Sir, while they are still available, strategic real estate, preferably uninhabited, move in and stay there, just squat there, till we need 'em.

NITZE: 'Buy land – they ain't making it any more'.

STU: I am sorry Sir?

MOORER: Mark Twain.

STU: Having found the right location, we proceed to develop 'austere facilities' there and wait till we need 'em.

NITZE: And where do you have in mind for your island-squatting dream?

STU: We made a list Sir, working on the criteria that they should be relatively small, of little political or economic importance, and sparsely populated. *(We could see the list, slide projector.)* And we have prioritised on the basis of airstrip and anchorage potential.

NITZE: I thought we were talking austere facilities.

MOORER: You never know what you might need further down the line.

STU: In the end we've narrowed it down to Diego Garcia, Agalega, Aldabra, Farquahar –

NITZE: Where in tarnation is Abracadabra?

STU: Aldabra, Sir, it's in the Indian Ocean Sir –

MOORER: They are –

STU: – there's only really turtles on Aldabra, the British Air Force have already shown an interest in basing some planes there.

MOORER: Huge turtles, like something out of the Lost World.

NITZE: What about the natives?

STU: There's probably more turtles than people in Aldabra, Sir.

MOORER: That was another consideration when choosing, Mr Secretary – we don't want any indigenous people kicking up a ruckus. Diego Garcia is part of the Chagos Islands, which in turn are part of Mauritius, there are just a few ex-slaves working the plantations, on a contract basis.

NITZE: These 'Chagos' islands belong to Mauritius?

MOORER: British call them the Oil Islands, they lease them to a couple of commercial companies.

NITZE: There's oil?

STU: Only coconut oil, so far…

NITZE: That might have swung it. So how far have we got?

STU: The Brits seem happy to come on board, Sir.

MOORER: Though they do expect to take some flak about the turtles.

NITZE: The Brits do like their animals.

STU: I like animals, Sir – I have two Springer spaniels.

MOORER: I never had you down as a dog man Barber.

STU: I love dogs Sir.

NITZE: Beautiful coats, Springers.

STU: Glossy as hell.

NITZE: Hm. Well we know how keen the Brits are to punch above their post-colonial weight. I am sure we can work something out.

NITZE: Good work gentlemen, leave it with me – I will take it to Mr Kennedy. Thank you very much indeed.

STU: My pleasure Sir.

MOORER: Thanks Mr Secretary.

NITZE: What are they called, your Springers?

STU: Rodgers and Hammerstein.

NITZE: That's nice. I loved *South Pacific.*

Exiting, STU and MOORER join in singing 'Happy Talk'.

SCENE 5
Caption: Crawley June 2005

The TEACHER is addressing a community group, in audience.

TEACHER: Thank you for coming, it is wonderful to see so
many younger folk here, many of you who have never
known your parents' or grandparents' homeland, you
for whom home is now Crawley – it is important to
understand your culture and to know your language,
language carries everything, it frees us and shapes us.

You young ones especially need to know Kreol, in case
any of you is ever lucky enough to go back *Laba.* Your first
word – *Laba* – out there. *Laba* – *(They repeat.)*

First, to correct a common misapprehension – Kreol is
not a sub-language, an argot or slang. Nor is it a pidgin – a
language to do business in.

Kreol is the language of the survivor, the language of the
rebel, of the undigested colonised.

Colonial literature ignores Kreol or doesn't understand it,
For instance, Robinson Crusoe uses foreigner talk to teach
Man Friday:

He shows extract from Mickey's Man Friday.
http://www.youtube.com/watch?v=VqRtMgOZuPA

MICKEY: You Friday, me Mickey.

FRIDAY: You Friday, me Mickey.

MICKEY: No, you Friday, me Mickey.

FRIDAY: You Friday, me Mickey.

MICKEY: ...aw, skip it.

FRIDAY: Aw skip it.

TEACHER: But Man Friday doesn't evolve a Kreol, he just ends up speaking really bad English. Which doesn't matter to Robinson, as Man Friday, having been saved by Crusoe, is forever after his lifelong servant, always dependable and completely obedient – the perfect colonial conquest.

'You taught me language', says Caliban in Shakespeare's *Tempest*, 'and my profit on't is I know how to curse'.

To curse – *Zurer.*

GROUP: *Zurer.*

TEACHER: I miss my Kreol. I miss *Laba.* I feel *Sagren.*

Sagren – your most important Kreol word. It is untranslatable. It expresses the sadness and loss we feel when we think of *Laba.* A physical sickness.

Let us listen to our first witness, Madame Lisette Talate, our first witness – we could say she is one of the mothers of the nation –

Listen to her tone, suffused with *Sagren.* –

SCENE 6

LISETTE TALATE.

MRS TALATE on video in Kreol, interviewed by the teacher of language. She then becomes a live actor.

TEACHER: Kuma ou apele?

MADAME: Lisette.

TEACHER: Lisette kuma?

MADAME: Talate.

TEACHER: Lisette Talate?

MADAME: Yes.

TEACHER: What was your mother's name?

MADAME: Marie Julia Bottezan.

TEACHER: Marie Julia?

MADAME: Bottezan.

TEACHER: Bonnesan?

The actress speaks in English, with video and sound.

MADAME: Bottezan.

TEACHER: Bottezan?

MADAME: Yes.

TEACHER: And your father?

MADAME: Arthur Talate.

TEACHER: Arthur Talate. You know about your mother and father. Eski ou kapav al pli lwin ki sa. Ou granper.

Video is gone, just the actress now, in English.

MADAME: I know from my mother that my grandfather was born on Peros Banos. My grandmother is Juliet. I was born on Peros. I know of my great-grandmother and great-grandfather but I know my grandfather's name. His name is Arthur Bottezan, as my mother is Marie Julia Bottezan. She was born on Peros Banos. As to my father's lineage, some were born on Salomon, some on Trois Frères. My father was born on Trois Frères. So my lineage was born on the islands. Monn ne laba.

A bell is rung. Key words are repeated in kreol (bold) and chorused by class of learners. We see some actions live, we see archive footage.

MADAME: *Laba.* In the morning the Bell-Call rings, we answer the call, the Master allots work to each of us, masters were all whites from Mauritius, working there on contract, Administrateurs, and they had assistants who were born out there and we called them Commandeurs. We answered the Bell-Call, the Master allotted us work.

There were 32 jobs out there. 32 jobs for men, women and children.

TEACHER: 32 different types of work?

MADAME: Men have to peel coconuts, dry coconuts; it's called **peeling**. *(Kreol word, with stress on second syllable, the class repeats it.)* The coconuts had to be collected first from muddy ground. Women then have to shell the coconuts. We were given 700 coconuts for a day's work *laba...*

TEACHER: 700 cocos?

MADAME: 700 coconuts dan enn ta – one by one we had to shell them... There are children working as helpers...the men had to go fishing...fishing is their work...then to build houses...thatched houses were built in Diego...and wood and iron-sheets houses too...

TEACHER: Ki laz ou ti kumans travay.

MADAME: When I was nearly fifteen, my mother allowed me to work...many women started working younger... I was a bit spoilt.

TEACHER: Ki travay ou ti fer laz kinz an.

Extracts of Imperial War Museum film of work, projected onto set.

MADAME: Every kind of work! Shelling coconuts, **tabalti**,

TEACHER: *(With Class.)* Tabalti

MADAME: cutting straw, filling coconuts into bags, turning **bastin**,

TEACHER: Bastin

MADAME: the Master sent me to collect **tek-tek** from the sea for him to eat, I did it and earned a day's work.

TEACHER: tek-tek

MADAME: The Master sent me to dig for **betay**... I did it...

TEACHER: betay

MADAME: There was no work I didn't do. I am happy to go to work...

TEACHER: You start at what time?

MADAME: After the 7 o'clock bell.

TEACHER: And you stop at what time?

MADAME: We decided! We used to stop at ten or half past ten if we could. I finish working I go home. I have to do my housework, wash my clothes, clean my house. I have to look after my children.

TEACHER: When you were a child did you play games?

MADAME: All children play!

TEACHER: Ki ou ti zwe?

MADAME: At dolls…we had puppets…we made dresses for our puppets and we played puppets together…we built houses…we cooked food…we had swings, we swang…

TEACHER: Was there anything you sang while playing?

MADAME: Of course like everywhere.

TEACHER: Do you remember any of those songs?

MADAME: No.

TEACHER: Nothing at all?

MADAME: I don't remember!

TEACHER: Not a single line? Not a single word?

MADAME: When I grew up I forgot all those things.

TEACHER: Nothing?

Now she is suddenly tired of him, tired of the questions.

MADAME: Laba we were at ease? I worked, I received my ration. Am I not at ease? I am in good health, no blood pressure, diabetes, cyclone… Laba I am in Paradise. I get up in the morning, I work, I finish working… I sit down with a friend… I play…those who want to fish just go out to fish… Am I not at ease? Am I not in Paradise? Laba every five years you hear about an old one's death… Here there's a death every day. Marriage there, death here. Am I not in Paradise? Hum!

And just when we were growing old a ship came and just took us away and threw us on a foreign land… Have I not lost my paradise? When I was young is one thing, when I grew up is something else.

PROSPER enters his counselling session.

MADAME: *Mizer.*

TEACHER: *Mizer* – that means misery, poverty. *Mizer.*

CLASS: *Mizer.*

MADAME: When *mizer* takes over, I can only think I am in *mizer*…though I played as a child I cannot think of playing now…my *mizer* comes first…my problems come first…my native land comes first… I feel so angry everyday I can't enjoy anything… I feel *sagren.* Ca c'est *mizer.*

SCENE 7A
Caption: LONDON September 2005

They know each other better.

PROSPER: That's it basically. Just empty. Missing something. Don't know what.

COUNS: And what is happening with your housing situation these days?

PROSPER: There are people planning things, behind closed doors, things which affect me.

COUNS: Behind closed doors – at the council?

PROSPER: Who knows – it could go right to the top, these things usually do, right to the top man, the top lady.

COUNS: Who is/the top lady –

PROSPER: The Queen, Tony Blair, George Bush, they're all in it.

COUNS: In your fantasy, the Queen/ is directing your fate.

PROSPER: Fantasy?

COUNS: It's a word we use, I could say 'dream'.

PROSPER: It's no dream. You try being evicted.

COUNS: I am just trying to understand. So you think people in government are making plans for you.

PROSPER: The plans ain't for me, the plans are for them, of course, don't you see, the plans are always for them, the elite protects the elite, but I am involved, we all are.

COUNS: What part do I play?

PROSPER: Don't know yet, do I – only met you a few times now.

Pause.

COUNS: What have you been doing since we last met?

PROSPER: Checking on me?

COUNS: I haven't seen you for a few weeks now.

PROSPER: I been in the library, got a book on Diego Garcia, where I am from. Sounds beautiful.

COUNS: So what's it like – ?

PROSPER: In the book, they call it Limuria, the peaks of Limuria.

COUNS: It has so many names.

PROSPER: Limuria is the mountains connecting Africa to Asia, before the world broke into pieces. The islands are like the peaks, the whole mountains are underneath, it's all connected.

COUNS: Go on.

PROSPER: First there was no one there, just turtles and crabs and reef, then the French took it, and put leper people there, then the British took it, then it was part of Mauritius. Certain people rent it and make coconut plantations. Back in slavery times it must have been hard, brothers come from Africa, working on these plantations, but later it sounds like a good life.

COUNS: Quite a history. So do you feel 'connected' to Limuria even? To the motherland?

Pause.

PROSPER: I suppose... She came back once, I wasn't there, must've been at school, left me something.

COUNS: The woman you called your mother.

PROSPER: At the commune, left it with the elders there. A chest, like a little treasure chest, said it was my Dad's, said to give it me when I was older, with a letter. They forgot it, too stoned probably, till they were packing up after the raid.

COUNS: What was/ in it?

PROSPER: Nothing. No treasure. A machete – like they must have used to chop the coconuts. Anything else was gone.

COUNS: And the letter?

PROSPER: Gone too.

COUNS: That must have been disappointing. And you haven't found anything more about her?

PROSPER: I have a name in my head from somewhere. Claudette.

COUNS: Claudette.

PROSPER: Don't know if it's her. Citizens Advice said check out births and deaths, there is a Public Records Office that's where all the papers from *(Posh voice.)* 'the colonial office' are, go there when I have time.

COUNS: OK – *(She checks her watch.)*

PROSPER: I had a dream about 'the colonial office' – and the dogs again.

Low flying airplane noise.

COUNS: We are actually over time, but I could do a little longer today if you wanted…

PROSPER: I'm gone. *(He exits rapidly.)*

COUNS: *(After him, but knowing he's gone.)* What about the dogs?

Back to memo recorder, some of this maybe a recording:

I suppose I got a little bit hooked. Fairly basic counter-transference, because of my own lost children – my miscarriages, pre-counselling – so, novice that I was, I researched possible dream meanings of dogs – all pretty hackneyed, dogs are intuition, dogs are loyalty, fidelity, protection – everything Prosper was lacking basically. And when I was on the internet I just followed through to the rest of that history...it's all there, I couldn't help it... To be involved or not to be involved?

SCENE 7B

Back to MADAME TALATE.

Either actor or film or both overlapping, or subtitles.

TEACHER: What about the dogs?

MADAME: I had six children on the islands and they had three dogs...my mother had dogs too...we loved our children and we loved our dogs...we feed our dogs like we feed our children...our dogs there were not wild...they were used to people...sociable...when we reached Mauritius I lost two of my children in 8 days...and the older one...he always talked about his dog...even when we had been in Peros... he talked about his dog...asking if we would go back to Diego to see his dog...till finally he fell ill...and died... *sagren.*

SCENE 8A
Caption: The Army and Navy Club, London, February 1964

JEFFERY KITCHEN, American diplomat, is sitting waiting. E.H. PECK, British civil servant, enters.

PECK: I am Peck, you must be Kitchen.

KITCHEN: Call me Jeff – good to meet you Peck, put a face to the name.

PECK: How was the flight, you must be tired, I hope you haven't been waiting too long.

KITCHEN: No, no, they weren't so keen to let me in, I dropped your name.

PECK: Members only I am afraid.

KITCHEN: Very olde world.

PECK: That's us. So… It's unusual to meet without an official…

KITCHEN: Just thought it might be useful if we chewed the fat a little, man-to-man so to speak, ahead of the official meetings – it's nice and quiet here.

PECK: Yes, you can usually rely on the Army and Navy.

WAITER arrives.

PECK: Jonathan.

KITCHEN: Bourbon.

WAITER: We have Scotch whisky Sir.

KITCHEN: Whisky then – on the rocks.

WAITER: On the rocks, Sir.

WAITER goes.

KITCHEN: So, why am I here?

PECK: Assuming no existential bent to your question…?

KITCHEN: Beg pardon?

PECK: Our understanding is that Mr McNamara has sent you to visit us, in the light of our special relationship, with a view to prosecuting an agenda, involving the detachment of the Chagos Islands from Mauritius and Aldabra from the Seychelles.

KITCHEN: In a nutshell – a coconut shell maybe.

PECK: Might one ask why this has suddenly acquired such urgency?

KITCHEN: The whole area from Suez to Singapore is heating up. We have the Paks starting to play footsie with the Russians, Nyerere in Tanzania with our friends the Chinese, Zanzibar. It's getting outta hand –

PECK: Quite so.

KITCHEN: – and now you're winding down, pulling outta Aden/

PECK: Simply can't afford it any more. Nuclear is the future for us.

KITCHEN: For sure, we sympathise. But the Persian Gulf is pretty key to us.

PECK: Oil.

KITCHEN: Where else are we gonna get it that cheap? So, we believe the answer may lie in the creation of a small naval task force, permanently stationed in the Indian Ocean, serviced by a shared austere communications facility on an island such as… Diego Garcia.

PECK: Austere communications facility – very elegant.

KITCHEN: And your RAF boys are interested in Aldabra.

PECK: If the turtles let us.

KITCHEN: Turtles shouldn't put up too much of a fight.

PECK: May I respond?

KITCHEN: That's what I am here for.

PECK: Aldabra belongs to the Seychelles, which are ours, and the Seychellois seem quite keen on starting a tourist industry, so an aeroport should keep them happy.

KITCHEN: An airport, perfect.

PECK: The Chagos islands are currently leased to a commercial company harvesting the copra, the coconuts, Moulinie and Co, with whom we are confident of doing a deal.

KITCHEN: Sounds good.

PECK: Ultimately of course the Islands belong to Mauritius, which is also ours and with whom we are already in negotiations regarding the possibility of their independence.

KITCHEN: That gives us an edge.

PECK: Not so. *Pace* the UN, one is not to 'dismember' a territory prior to rendering it independent. And when the idea has been floated thus far, the future president, Mr Seewoosagur <u>Ram</u>goolam, has demanded vast rental fees in return.

KITCHEN: Perhaps Mr Sss – Ram<u>goo</u>lam would like an airport too.

PECK: Mauritius already has an aeroport. Ramgoolam will need a platinum handshake and a knighthood to boot.

KITCHEN: So Mauritius might be more expensive.

PECK: Especially if the plan requires us unceremoniously to dump a few hundred natives from Diego Garcia on their doorstep. *(Beat.)* I don't suppose your chaps might consider employing a few of them on the 'austere facility', soften the blow so to speak?

KITCHEN: Read the plan. *(Handing over document.)* We want it swept clean, totally sanitised, don't care how you do it. They absolutely must go.

The drinks arrive.

WAITER: Scotch – on the rocks, Sir.

KITCHEN: Thank you.

SCENE 8B

MADAME TALATE.

TEACHER: Your father saved the lives of many people whose ship ran aground on the rocks…?

MADAME: It was on the reef not the rocks…at Six-Îles and Trois Frères there were reefs…that formed tidal waves… the captain had lost control of his ship…and got stuck on the reefs. My father was at Six-Îles…and he saved their lives. He tied a rope to the boat and then tied it to a coconut tree, then he pulled it along and saved their lives. So I was told…I was not yet born then. And the ship was called the Diégo.

SCENE 8C

Caption: The Public Records Office, Kew, October 2005

PROSPER is at the front desk, met by an official.

PROSPER: They told me to come here – I am looking for my mother.

OFFICIAL: You won't find her here mate – Have you tried Somerset House – we're more national than personal history, Public Records, Cabinet papers and the/ like

PROSPER: I know – they sent me here, my mother was born on the Chagos Islands.

OFFICIAL: Gotcha – you're not the first – sit yourself down there, it takes a while.

SCENE 8D

Back to Army and Navy.

PECK: *(He has been reading the document.)* If we were to adopt the perception that there were no permanent inhabitants, no belongers, simply floating contract workers, then there would be no population whose democratic rights needed to be observed.

KITCHEN: I love your British logic.

PECK: Thenceforward it would be a matter of maintaining the fiction. People must be induced to leave voluntarily rather than forcibly transferred.

KITCHEN: We would leave that entirely to you.

PECK: And is the delicate matter of our own finances…

KITCHEN: If we were to come to an arrangement regarding the British contribution to the development costs of the Polaris project – all of which is likely to remain top secret anyway –

PECK: I imagine HMG would be very receptive to such an arrangement.

KITCHEN: Well – we are on the same page then.

PECK: Good – so, Jeff – since we've saved the world from communism, perhaps we deserve a spot of lunch, what. The Army and Navy do a very fine Shepherd's Pie.

KITCHEN: Shepherd's Pie, Mr Peck – how could I resist!

SCENE 8E

Back to the Public Records Office.

PROSPER is in the Public Records Office, who may have fallen asleep at desk.

OFFICIAL: *(Bangs down box.)* There's quite a bit to wade through. Start with these – Cabinet Office papers from 1965 – see how you go.

Airplane noise again.

SCENE 9A
Caption: Gatwick Airport, November 2005.

CONSERVATIONIST is listening to headphones, standing in queue. The TEACHER is doing day-job as queue attendant.

TEACHER: Any knives or scissors, Sir?

CONSERV: *(He does so.)* Is it just me, or is this queue entirely stationary?

TEACHER: I am sorry?

CONSERV: Can I change queues?

TEACHER: If you change queues you have to go to the back again.

CONSERV: This is ridiculous.

TEACHER: I am sure it will start moving again in a minute, Sir –

What time is your plane?

CONSERV: 4.30.

TEACHER: You have loads of time/ you will be fine, Sir.

CONSERV: I am a nervous flier, I like to be at the gate in good time.

TEACHER: Apparently a woman tried to smuggle a dog through the X-ray machines.

CONSERV: Jesus.

TEACHER: Crazy lady. So they switched off the machine not to hurt it. *(To rest of queue.)* Any knives or scissors?

CONSERV: *(Answering mobile.)* I'm stuck in a queue, starting to get paranoid.

TEACHER: *(To queue.)* Is anyone supposed to be boarding in the next 30 minutes?

CONSERV: I'm already doing the deep breaths thing.

TEACHER: Laptops out of bags.

CONSERV: I'll ring you when I get to departures. *(Ringing off.)* Oh for Christ's sake!

TEACHER: It's OK, Sir. Take a seat. Where are you travelling to?

CONSERV: Mauritius.

TEACHER: Sir Seewoosagur Ramgoolam airport.

CONSERV: Say that again slowly?

TEACHER: Sir Seewoosagur Ramgoolam airport.

CONSERV: That's right.

TEACHER: Very nice.

CONSERV: It's for work.

TEACHER: What kind of work do you do?

CONSERV: Marine biologist.

TEACHER: You like the sea more than the air.

CONSERV: You can say that again –

TEACHER: The sea is my home…was my home.

CONSERV: Me too absolutely. I was in the city for a while, came back to marine biology quite recently, best decision I ever made.

TEACHER: Will it be your first time on Mauritius?

CONSERV: As I say, I am not a keen flier – ironically, it's a conference on conservation that I am flying to. That's why Mauritius, cos of the dodo?

TEACHER: Life is full of ironies. Check out Blue Bay, it's beautiful there.

CONSERV: Yeah I heard there's a good reef at Blue Bay – Are you Mauritian?

TEACHER: Not exactly.

CONSERV: You have that nice French singsong thing/ going on.

TEACHER: I am from Peros Banhos.

CONSERV: Is that in Mexico/

TEACHER: The Chagos Islands, a thousand miles from Mauritius.

CONSERV: Right, the reef, I read a paper on it I think, hear it's rather good.

TEACHER: It's paradise *laba* – it's paradise.

CONSERV: I'll have to google it – do you get back there much?

TEACHER: Never – I am not allowed. For me, it is paradise lost.

CONSERV: That's a pity/ why's that –

TEACHER: It's a long story. If you like reefs – Chagos is the best in the world – *(A dog ball bounces on from offstage – he throws it back.)*

Okay, the machine is back on – thank you for your patience ladies and gentlemen.

CONSERV: Good talking to you/

TEACHER: Bon voyage. Google Diego Garcia – and you'll understand.

CONSERV: Diego Garcia – will do. Thanks.

TEACHER: Do you have any scissors or knives?

SCENE 9B

Back to Public Records Office.

PROSPER gets another box of files delivered.

OFFICIAL: And another!

SCENE 10A

'An Exchange of Notes Concerning the Availability of Certain Islands in the Indian Ocean for Defence Purposes.'

In an animation sequence we see the sequence of exchanges of the British diplomatic service and the US equivalent between 1961–67ish, which will include the discussions around the awkward status of the 'contract workers', the need to conceal their existence from the UN, and the persuasion of soon-to-be knighted Seewoosagur Ramgoolam, Mauritian leader by Harold Wilson.

Prominent will be the sequence of 'Notes' exchanged between 1965 and 1987, each starting with 'I have the honour' and ending with 'Accept, Sir, the renewed assurances of my highest consideration'. Also the memo headed 'Maintaining the Fiction', and the famous 'A few Tarzans and Men Fridays' exchanges. Simultaneous with:

SCENE 10B

MRS TALATE.

TALATE: Americans. I've seen Americans there since I was a child. As a child I saw films they showed us…but all people in Diego knew…Diego belonged to the English… the English won it in battle if I'm right…since I was a child there was an English flag on Diego…they never stopped coming and going…there was a plane…the plane is still in Diego…everybody has seen it…when the plane first came, the island was not yet sold…then the war ended and the soldiers left…they left the plane behind…it had fallen down and…it is still there… I've known them for a long time the Americans…

SCENE 11
Caption: Diego Garcia, Christmas Day 1972

Plane landing sound.

ANNOUNCER: Ladies and Gentlemen, er… make that gentlemen.
If it's Tuesday, that means we're on Diego Garcia…
Fresh from an SRO crowd in Da Nang –
Misterrrrrrr Bob Hope!

Applause, cheers, whistles.

Enter BOB HOPE. He has stars and stripes outfit and a golf club. Every line is punctuated with applause and laughter.

BOB: I love the runway you have here. Great golfing country…even the runway has 18 holes.

No seriously you Seabees are doing a great job…whatever it is exactly you're doing, wherever it is exactly we are. Even the land crab has sworn to secrecy.

I hear you made this beautiful 8,000 foot apron from blasting the reef out there – did I say you fellas were blasting reefers – well you know what I meant.

Here I am to share Christmas with you, I bet some of you guys were afraid you wouldn't have a turkey.

I just dropped in from Phnom Peng city – they've got a Xmas truce for 24 hours – that's beautiful isn't it, a war with a commercial break.

I'm sorry you only got me – Mr Nixon's probably too busy, now he's back in the White House – he's been on a world tour too – he's learning to eat with chopsticks, he's doing alright with the rice but he's having trouble with the soup.

But really it's important we get along with China, because there's 800 million of them, which proves they don't spend all their time playing ping-pong.

And he's been having a little chat to nice Mr Brezhnev in snowy Moscow – brrrr – is that why they call it the cold war?

They couldn't find a Xmas tree for me to bring – so you'll have to hang your baubles on something else – Well how's this for a substitute – the wonderful Miss Belinda Green all the way from Australia, Miss World 1971.

Enter BELINDA GREEN, played by TALATE actor, in coconut shell bikini.

Nice tan Belinda, you look like you've been enjoying the sunshine.

BEL: I certainly have Bob.

BOB: Some people said I was nuts to come here – how are you finding it Belinda?

BEL: I like it Bob – if you can avoid the coconuts falling on your head.

BOB: Well you look like you found a novel use for the local crop yourself.

BEL: Do you like my coconuts Bob?

BOB: I certainly do Belinda

BEL: They are kind of neat.

BOB: You can say that again.

BEL: They are kind of neat – don't you think so guys?

Applause.

BOB: No seriously, I want to thank Secretary of Defence Melvin Laird for making this Christmas trip possible… Let's face it, we're still the Big Daddy of this world, even though *rapprochement* and *detente* are all the rage.

Would you like some *rapprochement* Belinda?

BEL: French food just doesn't agree with me Bob.

BOB: Nor me… Back in Vietnam I talked to a lot of our fighting men and even though Mr Nixon's decided it's time to bring them home, they're putting up a great fight…

and just like all 800 of you stuck on this rock in the middle of the ocean making something Mr Kennedy started and every Mr President since has carried on with… I don't think any of us ever had a better Christmas present, than you guys helping to save the world, we'll get you home soon.

Applause.

BOB: So what are you going to do for us Belinda?

BEL: Well Bob I was going to encourage the guys to take time out from building whatever it is they are building, and having a little R and R with me –

BOB: R and R?

BEL: Rock and roll!

BOB: Rock and roll with you – I should coco!

BEL: Are you ready for this guys? Well let's do it.

Rock and roll music, BELINDA takes PROSPER and twists with them, BOB shimmies along.

SCENE 12
Caption: Hotel Grand Baie, Mauritius, November 2005

Plane landing sound. CONSERVATIONIST on hotel phone.

CONS: *(He is googling. We hear the sound of video of US Navy promo for Diego Garcia.)*
   http://www.youtube.com/watch?v=uWYCcdiqsBA

Jesus –

(Phone rings.) Hi.

No all fine. It's lovely, hotel's great, only had one conference session so far, think I acquitted myself okay.

Most of them had name badges.

On the phone it's fine, I don't have to panic on the phone, face to face it's always a bit of a nightmare – like, who the fuck are you.

A woman tried to take a dog through the machines.

Yes, crazy. But then I started chatting to this rather sweet guy from the Chagos Islands.

I am not going to take <u>everyone's</u> picture, that would be bonkers, probably won't work anyway.

Yep – that's right – bang in the middle of the Indian Ocean – ?

I know, I am looking at it now on this YouTube site.

YouTube – people put their home movies on the web.

Don't ask me – can you hear it – it's all half-naked GIs and barbecues.

Apparently the yanks took it over like forty years ago, drove off all the people, and they don't let anyone in there.

Anyway by all accounts the reef there could be absolutely amazing. I dreamt about it on the plane. Thinking of trying to check it out when I come back from Mauritius, not sure how easy it is to visit.

Jesus –

Sorry, there's all these mad people making comments, you should see this.

Various of internet nutters enter and take up positions.

OK, well next time you could come maybe, I –

Let's see where it leads.

'kay – why not, if you are sure – make a baby – night then, sorry, morning, bye.

He continues to watch YouTube.

SCENE 13

Internet Debate.

This is a community participation element, to be played by different teams of Cardboard Citizens' workshop participants. Most of these comments appear projected, as on computer screen. Simultaneously incarnated by a number of weirdos of various kinds at computer screens in different parts of the world. Some in audience. Funny hats, cups of coffee, underpants, doing other things at the same time. They do not speak many of their lines, they may say odd words, sometimes whole lines – some of these lines are written in **bold***. They may go away, do something else and come back. Their lines are projected as typed, mistakes and all. Several things can be typed at once.*

At a certain point the video should change from the above one to:

**http://www.youtube.com/watch?v=
NDTCgay-5Cw&feature=fvw**

> *About halfway through the scene, some of the internet people merge from handjive into happy dance routine with the track which underscores the video referenced above.*

MICHELANGELI23: **Diego Garcia belongs to the Chagossian people** who were expelled and forced to live in inhumane conditions in Mauritius.

LEMURAI: **I was there in 92** for four days pulled in off of the USS Ranger. Beautiful island one of my best port of calls for some liberty.

GULFPORTER: **DG does NOT belong to the former slaves that were IMPORTED to the island** to work on the coconut plantation…

LEMURAI: **BeUtiful island** one of my best port of calls for some liberty.

GULFPORTER: it belongs to the same people that owned the island BEFORE they were brought there. also **its not a 'nation' its a territory**.

LEMURAI: That island is so beautiful in person **I miss turtle cove.**

SEYGIRL appears on a plasma screen, as if skyping.

SEYGIRL1: the slaves were not imported. they were captured from Africa.. **i come forM that region. I know whats going on**

GULFPORTER: **LOLOLOL**

SEYGIRL1: **the usa paid the brisTish for the island and expelled the people**.

GULFPORTER: There were no indigenous/aboriginal people of Diego Garcia.

LEMURAI: **I heard the people got compensated**

GULFPORTER: **Those people were no more indigenous to Diego Garcia than slave descendants are to Virginia**.

SEYGIRL1: You mean like ten years after they were chucked out the Bristish made the creole speaking people signed a document in english which none of them understood, renouncing all their rights for a few hundred pounds. **please open your eyes**.

TROUBLEDICONOCLAST: **so maybe we could kick out all white americans from the USA because none of them are indigenous to America**

MICHELANGELI23: Britain owns the island and is entirely responsible for depopulating it. America merely rents the land from Britain. **Some people on here are incredibly ignorant.**

GULFPORTER: If the US Navy wants to depopulate the island I live on so that they can build a naval base, **they can legally do that through eminent domain**. Those who own property will be compensated for it, and those who don't will simply have to leave. That's the way it works.

SEYGIRL1: Thank you for explaining this to some nuts people michaelangeli!! **My mum was born there and it would be good for me to be allowed to know the place she was born!!** As you know still fighting for it and its sad!!!!!!!!!!!!!!

ASCORBICACID1: **The British and American governments ought to be eternally ashamed.**

SEABOARDMARINER: **Thanks Royal Navy**. We've been number one since 1945 but that's because we know you have our backs! **Rule Britannia**!

DOGWITHNONAME: Didn't it help us win some wars guys? But **I heard it might get flooded with the see level rising**

TROUBLEDICONOCLAST: Yeah great, the B-2 Stealth Bomber and the B1-B strategic bomber used in Iraq were deployed from Diego Garcia.

CARISBONITA: **Mother earth is ill.**

ITZMRRICE: **Hey Ms. Hall this is Rice!!! I just seen you on the YouTube video** found this browsing…

GULFPORTER: Dontcha just love it. **The myth of the indigenous people**

ITZMRRICE: **I miss you all!!!**

GULFPORTER: of Diego Garcia combined with **the total bullshit of sea level rise** (there is no sea level threat to Diego Garcia or the Maldives).

Second video should have started by now, people at their screens start handjiving, then into full-scale dance routine, while the texts continue across the bottom of the video, comments section.

http://www.youtube.com/watch?v=NDTCgay-5Cw&feature=fvw

MANFRIDAY should enter around here, he and SEVGIRL remain at their screens till end.

MCHUME65: **Sometimes a military base is more important that a few coconut farmers**.

ASCORBICACID1: Yeah always better to kill then feed

TROUBLEDICONOCLAST: Why don't you just call them niggers? It's what you meant – isn't it. **I wonder if you would be saying the same thing if you were to be forced from your home tomorrow to make way for a military base.**

ITZMRRICE: **Hey Ms. Hall this is Rice!!!**

MCHUME65: WOW, that's deep! Since none of you has been to D.G., you can't imagine how 2000 people, 40+ years later, on that VERY tiny atol, would be like. **They would over populated, inbred, and starving.**

ITZMRRICE: **Are you out there?**

MCHUME65: They are too far away from anywhere to be supplied and they couldn't afford it anyway. **Sometimes you got to feed here and kill there. That's the way it is. Grow up.**

ASCORBICACID1: Yeah so you did everyone a huge favour by going there and kicking them off their own land. People where living quite well befire the UK/US turned up, its called living with nature, they dont need a bigmac or cola to live! **You grow up**

PROSPER starts posting: he speaks all his posts out loud.

PROSPER: Hi – ManFriday here, I am new to the Forum

HUMANLEAGUE002: *Comment removed*

MCHUME65: You are so in-credibly naive, I don't know where to begin. Should the UK have gone about differently, of course. But that was a long time ago. Many bad things happen in this world. Get a clue. Yeah, you don't a big mac or a cola to live, but you can't live off coconuts either.

LEMURAI: All I can say is to the people that were removed from the island… **I'm truly sorry that this happened to yall**; My thing is if it weren't for the island's strategic location, a lot of current operations wouldn't have happened.

MANFRIDAY: I am looking for my roots

TROUBLEDICONOCLAST: **But your not 'truly sorry', are you**?. Those people are the Chagossians and they now live in the slums of Mauritius and should be allowed to return to the archipelago in its entirety; with the military base removed.

MANFRIDAY: **I think my mother was born on Diego**

TROUBLEDICONOCLAST: **arsehole**

LEMURAI: I was there a bunch of times. I was briefed it wasn't anyone living here.

ITZMRRICE: **Hey Ms. Hall**

TROUBLEDICONOCLAST: **Gulfporter, r u indegeneous to where you ar e living now?? if no maybe we could kick u out as well...lol**

SEYGIRL1: **Hi Manfriday – I am from there too**

DOGWITHNONAME: Apparently, the first chagossians came onto the island in 1776, same year as the independance of USA...

GULFPORTER: **what's your point brainwashed dickhead..** why are you viewing this anyway...as i said you know shit so say shit and keep crap to yourself...asshole.

MANFRIDAY: Hello Seygirl – can you help me find my roots, I'm in London

ITZMRRICE: **maybe its not you, Ms. Hall**...

SVANGUNJAH: fuck you!!!! **Gulfporter you stupit ideot!!! Hijo de puta!!! verfickter voll ideot!!!!!**

SEYGIRL1: **Which part? I'm in Seychelles. There is a community in Crawley.**

SVANGUNJAH: these islanda were stolen from there people!!! **how dare you saying that they were "compensated for being displaced" with what 3000 pounds and a dokumend to be signed in Englisch** where they where giving up all there rights to the island!!! these peoble have be deported and fallacious deceived by the British goverment!!!

GULFPORTER: **lol...wat a laugh... u seriously do not know fuck what you are talking about.** where do your info comes from, i bet british/american sources... **brainwashed asshole**

MANFRIDAY: **Thats a pity. Crawley – I want to visit the Chagos, how can I do it**

SEYGIRL1: **LOL – You can't get to visit, didn't you know**

SVANGUNJAH: **Gulfporter!! you are some stupid untaught ignorant,** "bevor du deine dumme meinung sagst informiere dich erst mal richtig!!! = bevor giving up you stupid opinion inform your self right!!!! **imbecil de mierda!!! gente como tu es lo peor!!!!!!! wanker!!!!**

ITZMRRICE: **Look for me on Facebook, Ms Hall.**

CARISBONITA: Many Nations around the world have been murdered and exiled from their original lands.

MANFRIDAY: I read that yachts go there

CARISBONITA: Creator is saddened and Mother Earth is ill. When the day comes, when the waters will grow, the lava will set fires in places never before imagined

SEYGIRL1: Not Chagossians though

GULFPORTER: LOL

MANFRIDAY: **I keep thinking about dogs**

MCHUME65: With you there brother

GULFPORTER: **Who, who, who let the dogs out**

TROUBLEDICONOCLAST: Shut up arsehole.

GULFPORTER: Who who who let the dogs out

The dance routine is over, forum members are leaving.

SEYGIRL1: **It's all in the legal documents, check the files if you really want to know…**

MANFRIDAY: **Legal documents?**

SEVGIRL: **The fightback - Read the testimonies - gotto go now - good luck Manfriday - hope you fine your ma…**

GULFPORTER: **Who who who let the dogs out**

SEYGIRL1: **Fuck off Gulfport**er

CARISBONITA: World is unbalanced, Mother Earth is troubled and she is crying for us all. Only way to appease her is to meditate, to chant OM, Om, Om Om,

TROUBLEDICONOCLAST: **Lol Lol Lol**

CARISBONITA: **Shanti shanti shanty**

GULFPORTER: **Who who who who**

SVANGUNJAH: **Ruff Ruff Ruff Ruff**

SCENE 14

The Counsellor's room, December 2005.

They are laughing together.

PROSPER: And you think I've got problems Mary. Here's your laptop back.

COUNS: Keep it, we've gone mac,

PROSPER: Really?

COUNS: I'm glad you're over your phobia.

PROSPER: Thank you. There's some MAD people out there Mary.

COUNS: I know people who are writing whole theses on that – it's called deindividuation.

PROSPER: What's that?

COUNS: The effect of anonymity, when people can't be held accountable for their actions it's like other people don't exist, they become unpeople, faceless.

PROSPER: These people are animals, man.

COUNS: Tell me more seygirl stuff.

PROSPER: Yeah, right, apparently we Chagossians believe our home is where our umbilical cord is buried. The motherland.

COUNS: So maybe yours is on Diego.

PROSPER: On Diego, being trampled on by GIs. Can't believe England just sold the island to the Yanks. There are graveyards that go back 100 years or more.

COUNS: They were Catholics right.

PROSPER: *(Surprised.)* That's right.

COUNS: I guess everyone was Catholic in that part of the world.

PROSPER: That was all imposed from outside, they had their own beliefs, they had a death ritual called *aniwawoah.*

COUNS: *Aniwawoah.*

PROSPER: It's African right, probably Madagascar, when someone dies, for eight nights everyone prays, everyone mourns, and they burn candles and make offerings, then one person is chosen, the one with the spirit in him, he gathers up all the candle ends and stuff, and he sets off, and he mustn't look back, and when he gets to the middle of a crossroads, he dumps all the stuff there in a pile. That's our ritual.

COUNS: Where does this sit with Rastafari?

PROSPER: I didn't buy all that. I liked some of the Biblical texts, I liked Ezekiel raising the dead – but this feels more real, more me. I feel I'm getting closer to the truth, maybe closer to my mother, to finding my mother. Maybe I am…

COUNS: How does that feel?

PROSPER: Calmer? Connected, maybe. Next week I am back in the Records Office, there's a whole legal box, can't wait, it's the truth, the whole truth and nothing but the truth. /

COUNS: Don't get your hopes up too much – what if you don't like what you find?

PROSPER: It's make or break. Just a trace of her or me, a name, a picture, something. I am the man in the crossroads, 'cept I have to look back, otherwise I got no way of going forward.

I know. Our time is up. See you next time, wish me luck, Mary.

COUNS: Good luck Prosper.

SCENE 15

Caption: Depositions and statements to British courts, 1977, 1999, 2005

PROSPER is back in the PRO. This scene contains the intertwined and sometimes contradictory testimonies of MARCEL MOULINIE, in 1977, 1999, and 2005, MARIE THERESE MEIN, JOHN TODD, SEEWOO SANKAR MANDARY, and LISETTE TALATE.

MOULINIE: I, Marcel Moulinie of Mahé, Seychelles make this Statement in support of the application for Judicial Review herein, 1977, 1999, 2005.

MANDARY: Seewoo-Sankar Mandary Quatre Bornes, Mauritius. I first took up a post on Diego Garcia as a Government Meteorological Observer in or about July 1970. I knew Mr Marcel Moulinie, the resident manager of Diego Garcia.

MOULINIE: I also acted as agent of the BIOT Administration. This was negotiated by my uncle, Paul Moulinie.

MEIN: Marie-Therese Mein born on 3 October 1933 on Diego Garcia, both of my parents and all my grandparents were born on DG, as were my six sisters/ and five brothers. I lived at East Point, which accommodated the Administrator's house, a church with cemetery, and a medical centre staffed by nurses from Mauritius.

TALATE: I, Lisette Talate, was born on 19 March 1941. My ancestors have been on the Chagos Islands since 1830s.

MEIN: The Island also contained a coconut-processing works, which included a calorifier (where the coconut husks were burnt so as to heat the trays of drying copra).

TALATE: In the early 1960s, I had no reason to believe any misfortune was about to happen because we were living a normal and peaceful life on our islands. This is shown in a film entitled *Peaks of Limuria* shot in the 1950s – I am the woman hanging washing on a line in the garden of my home.

We raised chickens, ducks, pigs, turkeys.

MEIN: Geese, guinea-fowl, rabbits /

TALATE: We grew fruit and vegetables.

MEIN: Some of us had beehives.

TALATE: All of us knew how to fish from the plentiful lagoon.
The best lobster –

MEIN: Octopus –

TALATE: Crab, red snappers –

MEIN: and 'babonne' –

TALATE: for breakfast, lunch and dinner.
We made two famous drinks,

MEIN/TALATE: 'bacca' and 'callou'.

TALATE: When we drank these, we did not get headaches the
next day. We would drink and party every week. That is
how we used to live.

Maybe they dance Sega here.

MOULINIE: My duties were to look after the company's
interests and the welfare of the labourers.

MANDARY: All the land on the island was privately owned
by the company and all the people on the island were
employed by the company.

MEIN: My husband took charge of the shop and supplied
weekly rations to the workers.

MOULINIE: The labourers were simple people, not very
capable of looking after themselves.

MANDARY: M. Moulinie was the law on the islands.

MOULINIE: My position was rather like a father.

TALATE: When someone came of age, he chose a plot of land
and informed the Administrator and he would then build
his house / on it. The wages we received were low in
comparison to other countries. But it did not greatly affect
us since.

MEIN: We did not have cash economy there.

TALATE: In addition to the usual salary, all of us would receive one or two buckets of wine for our work.

MEIN: Which we could barter to those who wanted more.

TALATE: We never handled cash or money.

MOULINIE: I could terminate anybody's contract. I could transfer the labourers from camp to camp if I wished or to other islands. I kept a savings account for them so that they could save up money for when they went/ on leave. It worked very well. One tried to be kind, but could not be too kind as they would take advantage.

TALATE: Around 1964, we became aware of visits by British and US officials. We wondered why they were inspecting the Island.

MOULINIE: As agent I worked Mr J.R. Todd, the Administrator of BIOT.

TODD: I arrived in Diego on 23rd January (1971) with nine members of the US reconnaissance party.

TALATE: After 1967 we noticed that ships were coming less frequently with our supplies, notably dairy products and sugar.

MEIN: Rice did not stop at one go:

TALATE: First it started being dirty and bad quality – then it stopped altogether.

MOULINIE: I got on very well with John Todd. But the evacuation was not carried out well.

TALATE: The nurses and the school teacher left and didn't come back. The priest too.

MANDARY: Some families who left for the usual visit to Mauritius did not return.

TALATE: But why did they not tell their friends or relatives before leaving – ? – all their belongings remained on the islands.

MEIN: Early in 1970 my husband was summoned to a meeting with Marcel and Paul Moulinie together with Mr Todd.

TALATE: I had many friends who had left the Chagos for Mauritius for medical treatment or on holidays and whom I never saw again in the Chagos. They later told me that when they went to book a return ticket they were told that the Islands had been sold.

MANDARY: At the meeting they were given the news by Messrs. Moulinie and Todd. The Americans were very surprised to see several hundred islanders.

MEIN: They appeared to believe that the island was deserted, as they told my husband.

TODD: On the 24th January I told all the inhabitants that we intended to close the island in July.

MEIN: None of us had been consulted.

TALATE: A lot of people were very distressed and cried.

MEIN: My husband was in shock. He told me that if the Ilois did not leave Mr Marcel Moulinie had said that force would be used against us.

MEIN/PROSPER: On a number of occasions Monsieur Moulinie and Mr Todd made promises to the Ilois.

PROSPER: If they left they would be given homes, jobs and compensation.

MOULINIE: I said it was quite probable that they would be compensated.

TALATE: Men protested, women cried, children did not understand. One Chagossian, Marie Louina, died of a heart attack upon hearing that we had to leave.

MEIN: Just collapsed and died on the spot.

TALATE: Soon the coconut plantations were closed down, and all work ceased.

PROSPER: In May 1971 the USS Vernon County arrived with the Seabees, the US navy construction battalions and heavy plant and machinery. The Americans had to blow up part of the coral reefs to enable the Vernon County to sail up to the beach. All over Diego Garcia, we could hear the explosions and see tall plumes of water forced up into the sky.

Construction/explosion sounds start build.

MANDARY: One week after the arrival of the Seabees, all of the villages were completely flattened, including their graveyards.

MEIN: The whole area of Norwa became a building site.

MANDARY: The airstrip was completed by 19 July 1971.

MOULINIE: A number of ships came to take the llois away.

TALATE: When American planes or helicopters flew by, we used to hide in the house for fear that they had come to bomb us.

MEIN: My husband appealed on behalf of the Ilois, but Mr Todd said to him –

TODD: Do you people want to go the same way as the dogs?

MANDARY: Chagossians loved their dogs.

MEIN: Everyone had a dog – for fishing, for playing, for friendship.

TALATE: There were almost as many dogs on the island as there were people.

MEIN: Mr Marcel Moulinie, with the assistance of some Americans, went round the residential areas catching cats and dogs.

MANDARY: There was a programme of extermination of the Islanders' pets, The Americans started by distributing poisoned meatballs to the dogs.

MOULINIE: When the population began to dwindle in this period, one of the problems was the number of stray dogs, since it was common for families to have four or five dogs each. As the final evacuation approached, I recall receiving written instructions from Sir Bruce Greatbach.

MANDARY/MEIN: Destroy all dogs. STOP. Save horses. STOP. Greatbatch. STOP.

MOULINIE: By this time there were in excess of 800 dogs on the east side of Diego Garcia. I had to follow orders. I first tried to shoot the dogs, using US sharpshooters armed with M16s. It was often possible to shoot two or three of them, but the rest ran away into the plantations. I then experimented by poisoning dog meat with strychnine, but the animals which took this poison suffered so horribly that I had to shoot them.

MANDARY: I remember Willis who was an Assistant Administrator, found his dog Johnny, poisoned. Willis was extremely upset and carried the dead dog on his shoulders and confronted Marcel Moulinie and a group of Americans.

MOULINIE: I had to find a method for large-scale extermination, and hit upon the idea of gassing them in the calorifier. This is a small building in which copra is dried by burning coconut husks on the shelf below.

TALATE: Two military Land Rovers approached the building and backed up to bring their exhaust pipes close to the door.

MOULINIE: By luring the dogs into the calorifier with meat, and then shutting them in, it was then possible to gas them with carbon monoxide forced into the calorifier by revving up the vehicles' engines.

TALATE: They left the vehicles' engines running and went away. The calorifier had been converted into a gas chamber.

MOULINIE: After I had repeated the exercise a number of times I managed to destroy over 800 dogs and eliminate almost the entire population.

TALATE: We could hear the animals screaming in pain as they were burnt to death.

MEIN: I believe that these measures were taken to frighten the Ilois into believing that violence could be used if they did not leave.

We packed as much clothing as we could carry. There were about 35 men, women and children on my boat, leaving their homes and all their possessions behind. The boat was heavily loaded with the last consignment of coconuts.

MOULINIE: I obtained authority from Sir Bruce Greatbatch to leave on our ship with a cargo of coconuts. The weather was extremely bad, and after the vessel had been loaded Greatbatch told me to get rid of the coconut cargo. I was obliged to discharge a quantity approaching one million coconuts into the harbour.

TALATE: I believe the final evacuation took place in June 1973. I knew most of the other people who were on the boat.

MOULINIE: The horses were loaded on deck. Most of the labourers travelled in the hold. There were many more people than usual, including pregnant women and a cargo of copra.

TALATE: It was a 2500 mile ordeal to Mauritius and the ship had to stop in Seychelles, which increased the distance.

MOULINIE: The conditions of transit to the Seychelles, where I was waiting, were quite inhuman and the boat deck was covered in manure, urine and vomit.

TALATE: There was no proper bedding; no room to move and walk around, no toilet facilities so people were obliged to urinate and defecate on the spot and in front of others. People were vomiting on the floor, children were crying, there was no ventilation. The stench was nauseating and the journey lasted for several days. It was hell.

MANDARY: The horses were fed grass, but there was no proper food for the passengers throughout the 4 or 5 day passage.

PROSPER: I remember Christian Simon, could not bear the sadness of having left our lives and everything we had back in the Chagos; he threw himself in the high seas and disappeared in front of our eyes.

MOULINIE: When they arrived (in Mahe) there was no accommodation for them and the administration put them in the local prison.

TALATE: None of them had committed any crime.

PROSPER: *(Reading.)* Some ten days later, the Nordvaer took most of them on to Port Louis in Mauritius, to join those already there. They were dumped on the quayside, some of them refused to leave the boat. But in the end they had to, and they went to stay with relatives or friends, till eventually they were housed in a slum district outside Port Louis, living ten to a room. After some months a cyclone came, the first of many, and blew down many of their homes.

Cyclone kicks in.

MOULINIE: That is all I recollect about the affair. In my opinion the whole evacuation could have been carried out much better. For instance if we had paid the labourers compensation on the spot they would have been far more amenable.

In my opinion the islands could have been developed into a sound profit-making business despite the American presence there.

TALATE: I did not want to go. I wanted to live the rest of my life on Diego Garcia and be buried next to my ancestors.

PROSPER calmly closes the box of papers he is reading, and stands up in the library and screams. Blackout.

Interval.

SCENE 16

The Yachties' Blogs.

The stage is now much clearer, as if wrecked by cyclone. A wide and bright open space. Settings are now less naturalistic. We may be in PROSPER's head. People may stay from one scene into another.

PROSPER is practising how to use his machete on coconuts. PROSPER's comments are all ironic, not actual communication with the bloggers.

This scene can be illustrated with the snaps below and others.

Airswimming fish travel over PROSPER's head. Various yachting bloggers are distributed around the place, floating and blogging. ROLF and IRENE work at their blog together. The first couple enter, controlling their airswimmer and blogging.

IRENE: Day 25 blog,

ROLF: from Rolf

IRENE: and Irene

ROLF/IRENE: Fricke.

IRENE: www.castaway.com

PROSPER: Hello Rolf, hello Irene.

ROLF: We have been sailing the Indian Ocean in our 40ft catamaran.

IRENE: Castaway.

ROLF: To the almost legendary sailing world of Chagos – halfway between Sri Lanka and Madagascar, seven uninhabited atolls –

IRENE: Imagine this: the world around you water to the horizon,

ROLF: gently rolling, calm and blue,

IRENE: below a light blue sky dotted with pristine white clouds.

ROLF: The eastern horizon gets a fringe, of long, low islands,

IRENE: covered with coconut forests.

ROLF: You are in Peros Banhos atoll of the Chagos Archipelago.
If you had a bird's-eye view of the atoll, you would see a chain approximately 15 miles in diameter;

IRENE: The reef a green/brown thread in aqua waters, bejewelled with long, slim green coconut islands circled by narrow sparkling white beaches.

ROLF/IRENE: And, how can you get here?

PROSPER: Yes, how can I get there Rolf?

ROLF: Well, the only way is to sail: the Chagos archipelago, apart from Diego Garcia which is a naval base, is uninhabited and provides none of the usual tourist means of access.

IRENE: We had to obtain a permit from the BIOT authorities –

ROLF: (The British Indian Ocean Territories) –

IRENE: Which mainly entailed paying only an $80 fee for up to three months.

ROLF: Hi Eric, Hi Lynne.

ERIC/LYNNE: Hi guys.

PROSPER: – wow, it's getting crowded out there.

ERIC and LYNNE have been engaged in erecting a volleyball court or setting up a barbeque.

ERIC: Eric Toyer and Lynne Sands, Amarula:

LYNNE: www.amarula.com

ERIC: Almost 2 weeks out of Cocos we finally dropped the anchor in the Salomon Islands lagoon of the Chagos Archipelago. We were soon greeted by Benoit Renoir.

BENOIT: Benoit Renoir.

ERIC: Aboard the 53ft Chuck Payne-designed sloop.

BENOIT: 'La Tempète'.

ERIC: Who had been at Chagos for the past 3 months.

BENOIT: A'oy there!

ROLF/IRENE: Ahoy!

LYNNE: It is easy to see why this remote region is such a magnet for visiting yachts with its stunning islands and clear water, offering fantastic diving, snorkelling, fishing and a totally relaxing Robinson Crusoe-style existence.

ERIC: C'est un paradis, n'est-ce pas Benoit.

BENOIT: Salut, Eric, bonjour Lynne –

ERIC/LYNNE: Alright, Benoit?

BENOIT: 'ow is it 'anging Rolf?

ROLF: All ship-shape thanks mate.

BENOIT: Irene, you're beautiful!

IRENE: Ooh la la, Benoit!

BENOIT: The British claimed this territory about 40 years ago and transported all its inhabitants to Mauritius.

LYNNE: It's an unfair world Benoit!!

BENOIT and GHISLAINE are illuminated.

ERIC: Every few weeks a contingency of British Marines comes around to check out what's going on.

BENOIT: Our own private air show!

Planes fly low overhead, as in the first half, this should be reflected both in sound and lights, and people duck.

IRENE: We explored about 10 of the islands we're allowed onto.

ROLF: All the original plantation buildings, even the cemetery are derelict and moss-covered.

PROSPER: Some of my ancestors are probably in that cemetery, Rolf.

BENOIT: Tell them about underneath the waterline Rolf.

ROLF: Well…my, oh my… Wow… The corals are truly amazing: soft and hard, massive, healthy and of huge variety of type and colour.

ERIC: Tangs, wrasses, angel, surgeon, trevally and schools of parrotfish chomping away on the coral and also a giant manta ray.

PROSPER: Chagos sounds like all fun-and-games.

BENOIT: Well, it is, really; except when the wind picks up.

ROLF: – boy, you can get in trouble on the reef.

LYNNE: One morning we woke up to the gut-wrenching sight of two masts protruding out of the water at an angle of 45 degrees, next to one of the coral heads.

ERIC: The crew of a Canadian 60ft ferro-cement yacht had slept through the high winds and woke with the shock as they hit a coral head and the starboard side of their vessel was stove in.

ERIC/LYNNE: This is a sailor's worst nightmare!

LYNNE: Such an unfortunate tragedy.

PROSPER: It's a tragedy Lynne, it's a fucking tragedy.

ERIC: It was humbling to witness the humanity of all vessels in the lagoon, giving help, assistance and whatever moral support possible.

LYNNE: Though it doesn't detract from the devastation the family felt at their loss of their idyllic lifestyle and their 'home'.

SCENE 17

PROSPER with his COUNSELLOR.

COUNS: You hate these people.

PROSPER: I don't hate them.

COUNS: You blame them.

PROSPER: They feel no shame.

COUNS: Aren't you being a bit hard on them – they sound sorry.

PROSPER: If they were sorry they would do something positive instead of cruising round in their fancy boats and writing stupid postcards.

COUNS: So the world is divided up into goodies and baddies, friends and enemies?

PROSPER: At midnight all the agents and the superhuman crew come out and round up everybody who knows more than they do.

COUNS: That sounds like a good place to start from today.

PROSPER: It's a song –

COUNS: Who's the song by?

PROSPER: Everyone is telling lies.

COUNS: Why?

PROSPER: Keep the black man down, the white man up. There's nothing new – that's what the brothers always used to say.

COUNS: What lies?

PROSPER: I have been in the library, studying history and it's full of lies. When there are so many lies all around, how can you tell what is true?

COUNS: What do you think?

PROSPER: Why do you never answer a question?

COUNS: Perhaps I am trying to avoid telling you more lies?

PROSPER: There you go again.

COUNS: It's about boundaries / it's a methodology.

PROSPER: You stay mysterious, right, I never get to know what you think.

COUNS: Not because I wish you ill.

PROSPER: Who said you wish me ill.

COUNS: It's about staying neutral/ avoiding abuse of power.

PROSPER: Now who's paranoid?

COUNS: You said you have been in the library.

PROSPER: My people were cheated.

COUNS: And that makes you angry.

PROSPER: Wouldn't you be angry?

COUNS: We are not talking about me.

PROSPER: We never are talking about you are we?

COUNS: You came here to find yourself, you are our subject.

PROSPER: The Queen's subject – except that I am not, she didn't want me, I am a citizen of nowhere, because I have no papers, nothing.

COUNS: So you have moved from grief to grievance.

PROSPER: What's the difference?

COUNS: Grievance has an enemy, grief is just a hole to fill.

PROSPER: Yes I have an enemy, yes I am angry.

COUNS: What will you do with that anger?

PROSPER: I been to the library twice, and both times the same guy was sitting opposite me.

COUNS: So

PROSPER: So they're watching me, I am a threat.

COUNS: Coincidence?

PROSPER: If you like.

COUNS: For you its conspiracy.

PROSPER: You are a coincidence theorist. Do you keep notes on our sessions?

COUNS: Brief notes –

PROSPER: What happens to them?

COUNS: I keep them under lock and key. Nobody sees them.

PROSPER: Give me an example of a coincidence.

COUNS: Erm – They happen in my life – *(She almost blurts it out.)*

PROSPER: Is it a coincidence that the my people were taken from Africa and dumped on the Chagos, then taken from Chagos and dumped in Mauritius?

COUNS: That doesn't sound like coincidence.

PROSPER: Gran dimunn and ti dimunn.

COUNS: Teach me.

PROSPER: Big guys and little guys. David and Goliath.

Beat.

COUNS: So what are you planning to do with your anger?

PROSPER: I want to stop these sessions for a start.

COUNS: OK. How do you think that will help?

PROSPER: What's the point – I ain't any the wiser –

COUNS: If you want to stop, of course you can stop. But perhaps we should look at why you want to stop first –

PROSPER: Let's look then, but not today, cos I gotta get to court.

COUNS: What's happening in court?

PROSPER: Housing Association's finally evicting me.

COUNS: On what grounds?

PROSPER: You still don't get it do you? We live in parallel universes you and me. What does it matter why? They are evicting me because they are the the grand dimunn, and I am the ti dimunn…

Anyway I am afraid our time is up.

SCENE 18

October 2006, CONSERVATIONIST on the phone.

CONSERV: Hibbert, Edward Hibbert, I wrote to you about the possibility of visiting the British Indian Ocean territory. I want to apply for a permit.

No I am not a 'yachtie', I am a scientist, I know access
is limited and my visit would be strictly for scientific
purposes – I understood from the literature that there is an
exclusion.

That's right – professor. Conservation. Essentially I want to
make a survey of the marine environment, with a view to
establishing species counts, current levels of biodiversity,
resilience and recovery in individual polyps and whole reef
structures, after the damage done by El Niño.

El Niño. N.I.N.O., with a squiggle over the second N.

– An ocean warming phenomenon. It's Spanish for the
'little boy'. I've no idea, that's just what it is called.

I completely understand. I would be happy to be
interviewed by whomsoever.

British, born and bred. Yes I know about the history, I am
looking at it now as a matter of fact, and I wish to stress
that my mission is totally apolitical, I have no involvement
with any group or movement, I simply want to save the
planet, no more no less.

OK, I shall wait to hear.

SCENE 19
Caption: Mauritius – Crawley 2007

*The TEACHER is rehearsing a community play. The company are present,
seated, etc. He is instructing them.*

TEACHER: So when the audience arrive, you will distribute
copies of the petition, as if they were at the meeting.

*The following document is distributed to the audience, on paper as
if roneoed or typed en masse. PROSPER arrives, is given a copy of
petition, hovers.*

In English and Kreol on paper only.

We, the inhabitants of the Chagos Islands – Diego Garcia,
Peros Banhos, Salomon, have been uprooted from those
islands because the Mauritian government sold the islands

to the British government to build a base. Our ancestors were slaves on those islands, we are the heirs of those islands. Although we were poor there, we were not dying of hunger. We were living free. Before we were deported from the islands, the Military Chief who came there told us: 'Don't be discouraged; there is a large compensation that the British government will give to the Mauritian government to give you'. Here in Mauritius, when animals are debarked, an enclosure with water and grass is prepared for them. But we, being mini-slaves (human) we don't get anybody to help us… Many times we tried to ask the Mauritian government for a meeting with us. Many times we have written letters to explain our situation. We have received no answer.

We have decided to write to you, British government, to let you know our situation. We are not against your having bought the islands. We are not against your constructing a base there. We don't want to blame you. But we want you to do something about our situation. You British government, you must act on our behalf with the Mauritian government.

Here in Mauritius, everything is expensive. We don't have money and we don't have work. Here many Mauritians are unemployed. We have increased the number of unemployed. We have many kinds of problems that we would like to talk to you about. We let the British government know how many people have died through sorrow, poverty and lack of food and care. We have at least 40 persons who have died.

Bertin Cassambeu: Dead through illness, distress.

Ito Mandarin: Died after landing of grief and poverty.

Victorin, Michel, Vivil and Sabine Rabrune: Had no property, abandoned by everybody, died in disgrace.

Daisy Volfrin: No food for three days, died through poverty.

Joseph Kistnasamy: Burnt himself.

Syde Laurique: No job, no roof, drowned herself.

And many more.

And we the inhabitants of Chagos Islands, ask a favour to decrease our unemployed. Allow two or three persons from among us to go clean the cemetery where our forefathers, brothers, sisters, fathers and mothers are buried. We ask the British government to give us satisfaction.

PROSPER: *(Reading names to self.)*

The TEACHER has scripts in hand, as do a variety of young people and others.

TEACHER: Lalit.

The struggle. Which began with the petition, the British said it's none of our business, talk to the Mauritian authorities, and the Mauritians took no notice.

He notices PROSPER.

Bonzour. Qui ou nom?

PROSPER: I don't speak Kreol

TEACHER: That's okay, I don't speak Kreol –

He gets company to translate quickly, which they do.

ALL: Mo pa cause Kreol.

PROSPER: Mo pa cause Kreol.

TEACHER: Very good. Qui ou nom?

He quizzes an individual company member, who gets it right.

1: What is your name?

PROSPER: Prosper.

TEACHER: First name?

PROSPER: Prosper.

TEACHER: For us that is more commonly a second name. There is a very good family called Prosper.

PROSPER: I know – I found out – I'm not related.

TEACHER: Prosper – it makes me think of Prospero, on Shakespeare's island.

PROSPER: I am looking for my mother.

TEACHER: Full fathom five thy father lies – of his bones are coral made. Take a seat. We are rehearsing a community play with our friends here in Crawley about the mother country – and the struggle to get back there. *Lalit.*

The first of many legal cases. Michel Vincatassan, Can you read, Prosper?

PROSPER: Course I can read.

TEACHER: There's no shame in not reading.

PROSPER: I can read, I've read everything about our history, I don't eat for reading, all I do is read.

TEACHER: Then read the part of Rita Bancoult, mother of Olivier who leads our struggle back at home. *(He hands him script.)* We are in Port Louis, 1975. *(He now reads the part of MICHEL VENCATASSEN.)*

SCENE 19
Caption: Port Louis, September 1975

MICHEL: I thank you for coming to meeting tonight. I know how difficult it was for many of you to get here.

Most of you know me, but for those who don't, I am Michel Vencatassan, Commandeur, my family go back five generations on Diego, and I have news to tell you. But also here we have a visitor from America, Mr David Ottaway, who would like to hear our stories – *(Jeers.)* no let him speak.

OTTAWAY: Hi. Hi. My friend M.Vencatassan will translate.

MICHEL: Mo pu tradwir pou zot.

OTTAWAY: Look I am hearing some pretty bad stuff, I know you may be angry with my country, but I don't know what happened here, I just stumbled upon this story, and I really want to know about it, and I have to ask you to trust that

I will faithfully report whatever you tell me, a matter of which I assure you most Americans are currently totally ignorant. So please, fire away, this is a tape recorder, I wanna hear what happened to you.

MICHEL: Raconte misye-la.

RAM DASS: Mr Ottaway, my name is Christian Ram Dass. I am what they call Iles Ferme – I came from Peros Banhos to Maurice for a holiday in 1965, ten years ago.

2: That is what we used to do Monsieur Ottaway. Maybe once a year,

3: to buy clothes, to visit relations,

4: to holiday in the bright lights.

RAM DASS: When I went to the shipping agent to return, he told me the islands were closed.

RITA: I am Rita Bancoult.

TEACHER: *(Correcting.)* Bancoult.

RITA: I came to Mauritius in 1967 because my daughter Noellie hurt her foot badly when a cart ran over it. I took her to the hospital in Peros, but the nurse said –

2: Your daughter needs an operation, you must go to Mauritius.

RITA: So we wait two months for the next boat.

3: Boats would come four times a year.

RITA: And when it finally comes, with my husband Julien, and my five children, we sail five days and come in Port Louis. Straight away we take Noellie to the hospital.

OTTAWAY: How old was she?

4: She was three.

RITA: The doctor told us.

5: You have waited much too long.

RITA: And he operated right away, but it was too late. Gangrene took her from us one month later.

2:   God rest her soul.

RITA: I went to the shipping agents, Rogers and co, and the man there tells me:

3/4/5: *(Chorused.)* Your island has been sold. You will never go there again.

RITA: I have no words. I go back to the family, we were staying at the time with friends, but no words will come.

4: What happened to you,

5: what happened to you. Did someone attack you.

MICHEL: She heard every word they said, but for an hour her voice couldn't open her mouth to say what happened. Then she said:

RITA: We will never again return to our home! Our island has been closed.

MICHEL: Her husband fell back, his arms out wide. *(The community actors enact this.)* His sickness started taking hold. He could not understand a word she said. His feet did not move, his arms did not move, he was frozen.

4: It was a stroke, he died five years later.

RITA: Sagren. He died of sagren. *(She turns away.)*

MICHEL: *(Corrects pronunciation.)* Sagren.

5:   After Julian's death, Rita's son Alex lost his job on the docks, and turned to drugs and alcohol and died from overdose of heroin.

2:   Also Rita's son Eddy, he too died from drugs…

OTTAWAY: This is terrible.

3:   Many people here have turned to drugs –

4:   There is no work, there is only prejudice.

OTTAWAY: I am so sorry.

MICHEL: These stories are repeated many times Mr Ottaway, ours is a tragedy without end. When I left Diego, I was lucky enough to be able to take some things – And unlike most of us, I had a contract, a signed contract, and a birth certificate.

TALATE: You can't read Michel, stop pretending.

Ribald laughter.

MICHEL: I can't read, that's true Lisette, no more than you, but the lawyers can, and they looked at my papers and they say it proves that my father was born on Diego, and his father before him. So I am challenging the British government in the courts. In the language of the lawyers, I was 'ordered, coerced or compelled' to leave my home.

5: Déraciné.

1/2/3/4: Tenday, tenday *(Sounds like 'Entendez', Kreol for 'hear, hear'.)*

TALATE: I am happy to hear a man speak strongly. Since we came here many of our men have given up,

5: We women have had to lead the fight.

2: We men have been busy, trying to find work, but it's not easy.

3: So many of Mauritians have no work, how can we expect to get it?

2: There are no coconuts here.

4: When we put our children to school, Mr Ottaway –

3: If we can find a school to take them.

4: They are bullied, Mauritians call them Ilwa, for the teachers they are stupid, they are cannibals.

5: When the storm came and blew down our houses, we were moved again, they only gave us sheets of iron, build it yourself.

Pause.

TEACHER: Prosper… It's Rita's line.

It is RITA's line, but PROSPER cannot read any more, so TEACHER steps in and reads it.

Rita Bancoult. One day my oldest boy, Olivier, asks me why I am crying, and I tell him, 'The Englishmen won't let us go back to our land.' And he says back to me, 'Mother! One day I'll go talk to these Englishmen, and ask them why they won't let us go back to our land' – and I hope one day he will…

OTTAWAY: Madames and Monsieur. It has been my privilege to hear you speak. I will write up what you have said, and I hope that this will make other people listen in my country.

TEACHER: We will leave it there for tonight. Very good, you read well Prosper.

People pack up and leave.

PROSPER: You're the Kreol teacher, right?

TEACHER: In the evenings – in the day I work at Gatwick to earn money, many of us work there. And who are you, Prosper?

PROSPER: I don't know, I am looking for my mother. Is all this real?

TEACHER: We don't need to tell lies. *(Then in Kreol.)* Nu pa fo menti.

SCENE 20
Caption: Sept 1975/Sept 2011

STU is making a phone call, COUNSELLOR is making notes into Dictaphone.

STU: Admiral Zumwalt, it's Stu Barber.

COUNS: There then follows a period of rapid disillusionment.

STU: I am fine, thank you Sir, greatly enjoying retirement, busier than ever, I just wondered if you had seen the Post today.

COUNS: He came less frequently. When he did, he was more withdrawn.

STU: I think you will want to take a look Sir.

COUNS: And, I was pregnant and past the magic twelve – and paranoid about losing the baby.

STU: *(Reading.)* 'Islanders were Evicted for US Base' by David Ottaway.

COUNS: So I was easing down, trying to avoid stress, obviously.

STU: *(Reading.)* 'More than a thousand inhabitants of the Indian Ocean Island of Diego Garcia, which the Pentagon told Congress was virtually uninhabited, were forcibly removed. The islanders are now living in abject poverty here in Mauritius.'

COUNS: And I suppose I felt guilty about that. And guilty about all the stuff I had been reading behind his back – is that wrong?

STU: Well I can't believe some of this stuff, Sir, this guy must be a red of some kind…

COUNS: Guilty about keeping a secret of course…

STU: Well that wasn't strictly accurate, Sir, as there were <u>some</u> people there, we all knew that.

COUNS: In my heart of hearts I already knew I wasn't cut out to be a Counselling Psychologist.

STU: Yes, Sir, let's hope the folks in the House don't make too much of it. Storm in a teacup.

COUNS: He only made one appointment after that… I think he was sleeping rough by then.

STU: Thank you Sir, and the same to you. *(Phone down.)* Storm in a teacup.

Caption: September 2007

PROSPER: I met the brother again.

COUNS: The brother.

PROSPER: From the squat. He gave me a letter. The letter.

COUNS: What's in it?

PROSPER: I haven't read it. Not sure I want to.

COUNS: This could be the missing piece of the jigsaw – don't you want to know?

PROSPER: Will it help?

COUNS: The more we know the stronger we are.

PROSPER: Not always.

COUNS: Where have you been all this time?

PROSPER: You read it.

COUNS: Really?

PROSPER: Read it out loud.

COUNS: 'Boy, beautiful black boy.

I called you Prosper, because I wanted you to prosper, and I hope you have.

It is strange and difficult to write a letter so long before it will be read. But I wanted you to understand, a little of why I had to leave you.

I could not keep you, you were not mine, it would have been wrong. You will know I was not your mother. But perhaps you do not know that Brian also was not your father. Actually it was I who took you on, and Brian was my boyfriend at the time, and he made it possible to bring you back from Mauritius to England. He knew people who could help, he arranged for you to be put on my passport, he was good at fixing things.

But it's not so easy being a white and black couple in London – it's not black and white, to put it another way…'

And it went on like that, she made excuses, London not so swinging, difficulties, wanderlust, etc…

And then we finally discover the identity of the mysterious Claudette – but he was right, it didn't help.

And after I read it to him, he left. I only saw him twice after that.

SCENE 21

Caption: The Foreign Affairs Committee of the House of Representatives, Washington, November 4th 1975

Second caption: And Never Ever Again

Chairman Lee H HAMILTON (Indiana), Larry WINN Jr (Kansas), George T CHURCHILL, Director, Office of International Security Operations, Dept. Of State, Commander Gary G. SICK, Country Director for the Persian Gulf and Indian Ocean, Department of Defense. CHURCHILL and SICK are played throughout by the same actors. WINN and HAMILTON are played by a variety of actors. PROSPER in the Chair's seat. He speeds up and slows down the performance of this transcript as he pleases.

Maybe this is illustrated with slides. Maps, slum, people.

HAMILTON: Congress was glad to receive your report Mr Churchill, after Senator Kennedy's request, but in some respects, it begs more questions than it answers. So today we are looking forward to some clarifications from you and Commander Sick.

PROSPER: Commander Sick.

SICK: Mr Chairman, Diego Garcia is operational as an austere communications facility. A request was included in the FY 1974 supplemental appropriations bill for $29million for construction of expanded facilities to support the occasional presence of Navy ships in the Indian Ocean.

I am not sure how much you want to get into that – If not I will move with your permission to the area of the population transfers.

PROSPER: Yes, will you, please?

SICK: The entire focus, has been on the strategic rationale for Diego Garcia: why do we need this?

We focused on that element almost to the exclusion of everything else, and the statements which were made that Diego Garcia is uninhabited were considered to be simply statements of fact. That is all I have to say, Sir.

PROSPER: Mr Churchill.

HAMILTON: Is it the position of our Government now, that we have no responsibility toward these islanders? Is that our position?

CHURCHILL: We have no legal responsibility. We are concerned. We recently discussed the matter with the British. The British have discussed it with the Mauritian Government.

HAMILTON: It is our basic position that it is up to the British. Is that it?

CHURCHILL: It is our basic position that these people originally were a British responsibility and are now a Mauritian responsibility.

HAMILTON/WINN: We have no responsibility, legal or moral?

CHURCHILL: We have no legal responsibility. Moral responsibility is a term, Sir, that I find difficult to assess.

PROSPER: Congressman Winn?

WINN: Mr Churchill, where did you obtain the information for your report?

CHURCHILL: The basic sources, Sir, are British. Data from colonial days in Mauritius before it was independent.

HAMILTON: Did you at any point talk to the Mauritian authorities?

CHURCHILL: No, Sir; we did not.

PROSPER: Did you talk to any of the islanders themselves?

CHURCHILL: No, Sir.

HAMILTON: Were the islanders forcibly removed, as Mr. Ottaway reports in the *Washington Post*?

CHURCHILL: We have no evidence that any force was used.

HAMILTON/WINN: Did they go willingly?

CHURCHILL: Some of them were reluctant to leave, especially the older people. But they went willingly.

WINN: Under what kind of inducements?

CHURCHILL: When the coconut plantation was closed there were no further means of livelihood on the island.

PROSPER: So you cut off their jobs and then they moved.

WINN: Is that it?

CHURCHILL: The British closed down the plantation.

WINN: Have you been in receipt of this petition that was drawn up by the Diego Garcians?

CHURCHILL: I have not seen any such petition.

HAMILTON: Senator Culver described these people as living in a ghetto. The paper says some 40 of them have died, that they don't have any jobs – Do you know anything about the conditions of these people?

CHURCHILL: Apparently they are not happily settled in Mauritius.

WINN: Is it our position that they cannot return?

SICK: Yes, Sir.

WINN: We would not allow them to return?

CHURCHILL: That is right.

HAMILTON: The report also indicates that, your comments, Commander, that they are 'rotating contract personnel', seems to stand in contrast at least with what Mr Ottaway reports.

SICK: Sir: there is no question but that there were some people who had been living on the island for some time, for several generations.

The bulk of the islanders, however, the bulk of those who were there working on the plantations at the time, it is our understanding from the information that was made available to us that the vast bulk of them were there in fact on short-term contracts, the bulk working for the company who owned the coconut plantation on which they worked, the bulk.

PROSPER: The fact that they had a church there, that they had a graveyard there. They have written in their petitions about their deSire to lay flowers on those graves, that shows some sense of community, doesn't it?

SICK: It certainly shows there were people on that island for some time. Whether it was the same people or different shifting people is something that right now is beyond my ken.

HAMILTON: What is the role of Diego Garcia for the US military?

SICK: The role for which it is intended at this stage or after expansion?

WINN: How big is the airfield now?

SICK: The air field is 8,000 feet now.

WINN: That is pretty short.

SICK: Yes, Sir. It will reach 12,000 with expansion.

PROSPER: If you are enlarging the runway it looks like Diego Garcia is going to serve as a base for bombers and fighter aircraft.

SICK: No, Sir; we have no plans to.

HAMILTON: In the 1966 Exchange of Notes, paragraph 4 says, 'The required sites shall be made available to the US authorities without charge.'

CHURCHILL: That is correct.

HAMILTON: Where did the $14million dollars that we gave the British come from then?

CHURCHILL: Sir; this was a waiver of a fee that the British otherwise would have paid us. For research and development funds for Polaris.

WINN: Why did we give them the $14million if it was supposed to be a freebie?

CHURCHILL: We make a distinction between assisting the British in funding the establishment of the British Indian

Ocean Territory for which we did excuse a portion of the research and development funds for the Polaris.

HAMILTON: Commander Sick, on Page 8 you say, 'There was no indigenous population on Diego Garcia.'

CHURCHILL: The people, regardless of how long they had been there, were there for only one purpose, that is, to work on the copra plantation which was owned and run by a group that lived on another island. There was no other reason for them to be there. They had no other purpose.

WINN: Some of them have been there for three generations.

SICK: Yes, Sir; that is absolutely true.

WINN: I suppose you are correct, Mr. Churchill, when you say that **we** have no legal responsibility for these people. But it is certainly not a glorious chapter in the compassion of the United States.

PROSPER: Thank you very much, gentlemen. The subcommittee stands adjourned.

SCENE 22A

Desert Island Discs.

Caption: London, never

Music.

KIRSTY: My castaway today is someone most people will never have heard of – because he's a little person in the big world, ti dimoun en gran dimoune – Prosper, welcome to the show.

PROSPER: It's my pleasure Kirsty.

KIRSTY: Did I pronounce the Kreol right?

PROSPER: That was a pretty good stab, Kirsty, though I am new to it myself.

KIRSTY: For most people, the desert island is more of an idea than a reality, but you really do know about desert islands.

PROSPER: Well, it's become a bit of an obsession of mine, for obvious reasons.

KIRSTY: And you have become quite the historian, in your quest.

PROSPER: You know Kirsty, I am fed up to the teeth with history. I started on all this because this Counsellor lady told me it would help me find myself, find my mother maybe, but I am not sure it's helped at all.

KIRSTY: Why's that?

PROSPER: It's become a burden Kirsty, carrying this history around. All I want is to be free, to know who I am, just to live like everyone else, but instead I am an outcast.

KIRSTY: Well I hope you will share some of that history with us during the programme anyway.

PROSPER: I will do my best Kirsty.

KIRSTY: So what is your first disc?

PROSPER: It's a part of my culture called Sega. It's our music, they used to dance it on a Saturday, drink callou and dance Sega.

KIRSTY: What were the songs about?

PROSPER: Anything. Anything and everything. The day, the work, the masters.

KIRSTY: Let's hear a song.

Disc 1 plays, we see Sega dance group for two minutes.

SCENE 22B

KIRSTY: I should tell the listeners that while that was playing, Prosper you were right there, almost in a trance, as if you were back there. Laba.

PROSPER: When my people landed on Mauritius and the Seychelles, they had no way of making a living. So when the hotel trade took off, some of them, Mrs Talate and others, they made a little Sega band and went round the hotels to entertain the tourists.

KIRSTY: Very exotic.

PROSPER: At least it helped preserve the culture.

KIRSTY: So tell us something of that struggle, even though much of it must have happened before you were even born.

PROSPER: Well that's another thing, Kirsty, of course I don't even know how old I am. Anyway when they were all dumped on the quayside in Mauritius nobody would have taken any notice unless they made some noise.

KIRSTY: So what did they do?

PROSPER: The ladies went on hunger strike. Mrs T, Rita Bancoult. It was always the ladies taking the lead. They sat down in the park in front of the Embassy and wouldn't leave for days. They thought the police would be less likely to beat up a woman, but they beat them up anyway. Mrs Bancoult talks about grabbing a policeman's balls – she says for once <u>we</u> had <u>them</u> by the balls.

KIRSTY: She sounds feisty.

PROSPER: They're all feisty, Chagossian ladies, they were arrested loads of times. Rann Nu Diego.

PROSPER/TALATE: Rann Nu Diego.

KIRSTY: Which your Mauritian supporters read as, 'Give us back Diego', because they want the Chagos returned to Mauritius.

PROSPER: And we read it like 'Return Us to Diego', cos that's what we want.

KIRSTY: Which brings us to your second track.

PROSPER: Well it's a spoken word track, Kirsty, part of my historical obsession. In 1982, Sir Seewoosagur Ramgoolam held meetings with the British Prime Minister, and they did the deal which resulted in the compensation, a sum of £4million, which works out at about…

KIRSTY: £3,000 each?

PROSPER: Of course that was an important year for the British PM.

KIRSTY: So let's hear the Iron Lady.

Mrs THATCHER speech as if audio track, but performed by TALATE actor.

THATCHER: 'Mr Speaker Sir. The house meets this Saturday to respond to a situation of great gravity.

We are here because for the first time for many years, British sovereign territory has been invaded by a foreign power. After several days of rising tension, in our relations with Argentina, that countries armed forces attacked the Falkland Islands yesterday and established military control of the islands.

Mr Speaker, the people of the Falkland Islands, like the people of the United Kingdom are an island race. They are few in number but they have the right to live in peace, to choose their own way of life and to determine their own allegiance. Their way of life is British; their allegiance is to the crown.

It is the wish of the British people to uphold that right.'

KIRSTY: The Falkland Islands has two thousand people, five hundred thousand sheep and no turtles.

PROSPER: And I'm guessing the Falklands people are pretty white.

KIRSTY: I see where you are going with this, Prosper.

PROSPER: Anyway, when they offered the money this time, many people felt we had to take it.

KIRSTY: And this was in full and final settlement – your people all renounced your right to return or claim any further compensation or redress.

PROSPER: You've really done your homework, Kirsty. Most people didn't hardly know what they were signing. Lots of them were illiterate, many signed with thumb-prints.

TALATE: All of them were hungry, they had children who needed to be fed.

KIRSTY: Presumably you were one of those children.

PROSPER: Could be. So they signed, because they had to, because they were tricked yet again.

KIRSTY: So what is your next track?

PROSPER: Well a guy I know interviewed Mrs Talate a while back, and it took a lot, but eventually he persuaded her to sing a song, she hadn't sung for a long time.

Under next scene we hear MADAME TALATE's sad song.

SCENE 22C
Caption: December 1992, Arlington, Virginia

An old STU BARBER is writing a letter.

STU: To the British Embassy, Washington DC, December 1992

Dear Sirs, I am glad finally to receive a response to my letter. But essentially all you say is that the Chagos inhabitants never had any legal right to live there.

When I first dreamt up the whole Diego Garcia idea, some thirty years ago, it would never have occurred to me that the supposedly civilised UK would take such a narrowly legalistic position. It is devoid of the slightest respect and compassion for the human beings of a native society which had evolved over nearly two centuries.

Implicated as I am, I hope I have some right to a hearing. I am older now, and wiser I hope. I have studied the plight of our first citizens, the Native Americans, whom we also treated abysmally, and displaced from their territories, and I see some similarities. Now I have learned to imagine faces for these people, and in the papers I have seen some of the faces of the people from the Chagos. I am no longer blind to what I have been party to.

It is too late to undo most of the human damage. But perhaps it will help to allow and assist those evictees who still wish to, to return at least to the northern Chagos.

Yours very truly,

Stuart Barber

SCENE 22D

Back to Desert Island Discs.

We hear PROSPER iterating 'Hear the Word of the Lord' from dem bones.

KIRSTY: Why that last track Prosper?

PROSPER: I grew up in this squat with all these Rastas, and we used to read the Bible a lot, and I always used to love Ezekiel, when he makes the dead rise up. It's a song about making connections.

KIRSTY: So, where does this all leave you?

PROSPER: Well it's either fight or flight. So far I'm fighting. But many of our people committed suicide out of *sagren.*

KIRSTY: Is that something you have ever thought about? Is that an appropriate response?

PROSPER: You sound like my therapist.

KIRSTY: So take us back to the fight then.

PROSPER: Well for about twenty years that's it, till Mrs Bancoult's son Olivier made good on his promise, and started a whole series of court cases, based on the discovery that they were British citizens.

KIRSTY: So it's still not over.

PROSPER: It ain't over till the fat lady sings.

KIRSTY: Is the fat lady going to sing?

PROSPER: We'll see.

KIRSTY: OK, Prosper, so how do you think you would fare on the island, the British government seems doubtful that your people could survive that.

PROSPER: Kirsty, my people lived there before, there's 4,000 assorted Americans and Filipinos living there now, I reckon we would survive.

KIRSTY: OK, you have the Bible, *(She gives him it.)* so you've got Ezekiel, which you have already mentioned, and the complete works of Shakespeare, so there's *The Tempest, (She gives him it.)* with your namesake, what book would you take with you?

PROSPER: *Robinson Crusoe* by Daniel Defoe.

KIRSTY: You're thinking of that famous Foreign Office memo, 'Along with the birds unfortunately go a Few Tarzans and Man Fridays', meaning your people.

PROSPER: I think you'll find it's Men Fridays, Kirsty, I've seen the original document.

KIRSTY: I stand corrected. And of course Robinson is a great survivor, even before he meets Friday, just him and his dog.

PROSPER: He had a dog?

KIRSTY: Before he had Friday, he had his dog.

PROSPER: What was the dog called?

KIRSTY: I'm not sure he had a name. I'll have to look that up. And what about your luxury?

PROSPER: Well I would take my machete, it's from my Dad maybe, and it would help me survive.

KIRSTY: The machete is yours. *(She gives him it.)* Prosper, thank you very much for letting us hear your desert island discs.

PROSPER: No, thank you, Kirsty – and remember it's not over

KIRSTY: Till the fat lady sings…

SCENE 23

COUNSELLOR and CONSERVATIONIST, June 2007.

COUNSELLOR is drinking glass of wine, reading, listening to opera, a fat lady singing maybe? CONSERVATIONIST enters with case, and kit.

COUNS: Hey Mr Hibbert how's it going with saving the world.

CONSERV: Fine thank you Mrs Hibbert, I think we are getting there.

They embrace.

How's the little guy?

COUNS: Just gone down.

CONSERV: Hi Bruno/ how's it going fella?

COUNS: Please don't wake him, it took ages.

CONSERV: He's really filled out.

COUNS: People say he looks like you now.

CONSERV: He looks like a baby/ I missed you matey.

COUNS: To you maybe. The faceblind leading the faceblind.

CONSERV: So how's the life of leisure?

COUNS: It's a juggling act, even with just doing the odd session.

CONSERV: Well you know what I think.

COUNS: Anyway, come on – how was it?

CONSERV: What?

COUNS: Don't what me. The Chagos, was it all it's cracked up to be?

CONSERV: *(Excited.)* You cannot imagine. You just cannot imagine. Perfect. Just perfect. A reef made in heaven.

COUNS: Wow.

CONSERV: Pristine. That is the only word for it. Absolutely pristine. When we swam on the reef it was like entering another world. I didn't want to come back.

COUNS: Thanks.

CONSERV: No noise, no people, no stress, no pressure, just beautiful beautiful fish, coral like Henry Moores – Brain coral, you should see this brain coral, it's exactly like an enormous brain –

COUNS: No people? What about all the marines and GIs?

CONSERV: Hardly saw them, they keep themselves to themselves – and nowadays they act under strict protocols, long gone are the days when they would blast away a chunk of reef to make a runway.

COUNS: Since you got that dosh from the American Foundation, suddenly you are all pro-Yank.

CONSERV: It's there, no choice, they're not going anywhere. It's what the Israelis call facts of the ground. We have to accept the fact of the base and work with it.

CONSERV is fiddling with camera in fishtank – his face appears on screen as if seen through water.

COUNS: What are you doing?

CONSERV: Trying out a new camera...

COUNS: Does it ever occur to you that this American Foundation might have a hidden agenda?

CONSERV: Why does everyone have to have a hidden agenda, for Christ's sake they're just good guys.

COUNS: I'm a therapist, hidden agendas are us.

CONSERV: They want to save the planet, that's all, that's their only agenda, sometimes you sound like one of those conspiracy nutters.

COUNS: Just asking...

CONSERV: Sorry – *(Pause.)* Bit shagged out. It wasn't the most comfortable of journeys.

COUNS: So how's the 'campaign' going – Any progress?

CONSERV: Absolutely, I really think this lot understands conservation. I'm hoping to set up a meeting with one of Miliband's guys –

COUNS: Which one?

CONSERV: I don't know, his PPS or something, Peter something.

COUNS: No I mean which Miliband.

CONSERV: Oh, the smart one, the minister – apparently he is making really good noises.

COUNS: That's great.

CONSERV: This is probably going to be the most important thing I have ever done or ever will do in my life.

COUNS: Apart from…

CONSERV: Of course/ excluding young Mr B.

COUNS: Get your priorities right/

CONSERV: Seriously, this could be one giant leap for mankind. An unmitigated good.

COUNS: Well let's hope so –

Pause.

CONSERV: You're not still thinking about that patient of yours…?

COUNS: Client – I wish I'd never told you about him/ I shouldn't have.

CONSERV: I thought you were supposed to be able to insulate yourself from too much involvement – boundaries.

COUNS: Perhaps that's our problem in this world, too much insulation –

CONSERV: Come on/ love,

COUNS: It's such a weird coincidence, you getting into this whole Marine Protection thing, and me having a Chagossian on my couch –

CONSERV: I have heard a certain person suggest that there is no such thing as coincidence.

COUNS: Sometimes you are so dim –

CONSERV: I just think you've got far too involved –

COUNS: It's an injustice.

CONSERV: You're never off the bloody internet these days.

COUNS: It bugs me.

CONSERV: This guy is not seeing you for political solidarity, he's a patient for Christ's sake.

COUNS: Client –

CONSERV: He's not right in the head, that's his problem, not world history.

COUNS: Don't you see it's connected?

CONSERV: I don't actually.

COUNS: It's <u>all</u> connected.

Pause.

COUNS: Anyway, I haven't seen him for months, I just worry about him. Very vulnerable guy, not getting a lot of help. He can't swim.

CONSERV: You what?

COUNS: He can't swim. So he'd never be able to enjoy your precious reef even if he was allowed back there.

CONSERV: I think you should stop altogether for a bit, just concentrate on the little guy –

COUNS: Yeah, you might be right, I can hardly cope with the dual focus anyway – I just don't like abandoning people.

CONSERV: You are not responsible.

COUNS: Let's just keep telling ourselves that – we are not responsible.

SCENE 24
Caption: Southampton University, March 2008

CONSERV: We can't talk about reefs without paying attention to the humble architecture of coral reefs and the corals themselves. Corals are these really tiny atoms, they look like sea anemones, they build communal organisms with a common skeleton – they all depend on each other. Essentially all these tiny fragile little organisms connect together, they build on top of each other, and they form rocks. And the connections build, the rocks grow, just a few centimetres a year, and they become fantastic gardens, the most diverse ecosystems on the planet, and when they get to the surface they form platforms, and this is what the islands of the Chagos are – debris washed up by storms settling on top of coral platforms and becoming the fertile territory which becomes the ground for all those coconut palms and turtles and everything which is beautiful on those islands, including the beaches on which boobies squat and crabs scuttle.

Unfortunately, we are not looking after our reefs very well. What are the threats – Global warming, bleaching events like El Niño, tourism, and of course fishing. The most prevalent general threat is overfishing. Which is where the MPA comes in. The Chagos makes up one and half percent of all the world's reefs, ten percent of the reefs in the Indian Ocean. If we can make a no-take zone in this area, we will go some way towards –

PROSPER: *(From audience.)* What about the people?

CONSERV: *(Craning to identify questioner.)* This is something for governments to decide, not the humble scientist. All I can say is that the presence of human beings is certainly not conducive to the protection of species – sewage, toxins, pollution, / fishing –

PROSPER: Well there are some 4,000 people on the American base.

CONSERV: I don't really want to get into the politics of it –
all I can say is, we have a unique opportunity here, the
momentum is there, we should all get behind the MPA as
soon as possible, and then these wonderful reefs will still be
there in a hundred years' time.

PROSPER: Rann Nu Diego.

CONSERV: I am sorry?

PROSPER: No you're not.

SCENE 25
Caption: Mayfair, June 2009

*The CONSERVATIONIST is waiting at a table with his COUNSELLOR
wife. They are in an island of light.*

CONSERV: Shouldn't you be getting off?

COUNS: I'm fine.

PETER, A New Labour politician enters.

CONSERV: Please don't get into an argument –

COUNS: Why would I?

PETER: Professor Hibbert, I'm Peter, sorry have you been
waiting long?

CONSERV: No problem, very good of you to meet me

PETER: It's a nice change from people trying to sell us cluster
bombs –

CONSERV: This is my wife, she's not staying to eat.

COUNS: Hi.

CONSERV: She also has some knowledge of the subject, for
other reasons.

PETER: Intriguing. Anyway, I hope this place is OK, it's all
very retro, Shepherd's Pie and the like.

CONSERV: This is on the Foundation by the way.

COUNS: Really?

PETER: Very kind.

WAITRESS: *(East European accent.)* Would you like something to drink?

PETER: I will have a Kir please.

CONSERV: A Perrier if I may.

COUNS: I will have a gin and tonic, just to buck the trend.

WAITRESS: Of course.

PETER: So, Adam tells me you have some constructive thoughts about the Chagos Islands.

CONSERV: I hope so.

PETER: Well I took the precaution of a little pre-lunch update from one of our civil servants – so I am fully up to speed on the islanders front.

CONSERV: Possibly more than me, that's not really our angle.

COUNS: I've lost the plot with all their court cases.

PETER: This is where a training at the bar really comes into its own, Mrs Hibbert.

COUNS: Mary, please.

PETER: Mary. OK, a beginner's guide. Essentially in 1997, a rather enterprising British solicitor working with a Mauritian journalist discovered that the ex-inhabitants of the Chagos turn out to be British citizens, had been all the time.

CONSERV: They didn't know?

PETER: They didn't know, actually <u>we</u> had sort of forgotten, though it's pretty clear the Civil Service boys at the time knew perfectly well, and managed to keep it hush hush.

COUNS: Along with everything else/

CONSERV: Mary/

PETER: Along with absolutely everything else from knockdown Polaris missiles to wholesale canine genocide – not our finest hour, definitely.

COUNS: Agreed.

PETER: So, since they now knew they were British citizens, they had the right to institute public law proceedings against the decision to deny them the right of abode in BIOT.

COUNS: The Chagos.

PETER: Foreign Office love an abbreviation.

CONSERV: My lot are a bit like that.

PETER: This case is known as Bancoult 1, after a very determined electrician called Bancoult who heads up the support group in Mauritius, his mother was on one of the last boats out.

COUNS: Rita Bancoult.

PETER: I say, you're quite an expert.

COUNS: I remember people.

CONSERV: This was the one they won.

PETER: In spades. I can try to explain if you are interested.

COUNS: Please.

WAITRESS: One Kir, one Perrier.

CONSERV: Thank you.

WAITRESS: And a Gin and Tonic.

COUNS: Thank you.

WAITRESS: Would you like to order?

PETER: I would like the kidneys, followed by the hake – oh, is that wrong of me?

CONSERV: Well it's a tad threatened…

COUNS: I am sure we can let Peter off on this occasion.

PETER: It's all so complicated these days.

CONSERV: And I will have the soup and then the Shepherd's Pie.

WAITRESS: And for madam?

CONSERV: She's not eating.

COUNS: I'm not eating.

PETER: White or red?

CONSERV: Whichever.

PETER: And a bottle of the Saint Emilion, please.

WAITRESS: Thank you Sir.

PETER: Are you sure you won't/ stay?

CONSERV: We have a little boy at nursery.

COUNS: I have to pick him up.

PETER: Never mind. So, back to the legal status quo. You're aware of the legal mechanism used to create the BIOT in the first place.

CONSERV: The order in council.

PETER: It's wonderfully arcane. The Queen gathers a small group of Counsellors, they bow their heads and they assent. It's a way of getting round the whole parliamentary rigmarole.

COUNS: Isn't that how Mr Blair took us into the Iraq war?

PETER: Well spotted, yes that's the last time we used it, similar reasons, though more about hurry in that case. Anyway, the 1965 Order in Council empowered the BIOT commissioner at the time/

COUNS: Sir Bruce Greatbatch/

PETER: To legislate for BIOT's Peace Order and Good Government.
The question was, was it 'good government' for Sir Bruce to exile the whole colonial population from their homeland.

COUNS: How could it be in the interests of a population/to exile them?

CONSERV: Difficult to defend really.

PETER: No, no no, disgraceful of course, but you do have to understand the circumstances at the time.

CONSERV: The Cold War.

PETER: The Cold War, the balance of power – Give them the benefit of the doubt, these guys thought they were saving the world.

CONSERV: I gather the base has been pretty useful since.

PETER: For sure – post 9/11 it has been heavily utilised.

COUNS: Very handy for bombing Iraq or Afghanistan.

PETER: Well, badly, yes. Anyway in 2000, they won a victory.

CONSERV: This is when Robin Cook stands on the steps of the court and says he won't appeal, they can go back etcetera.

PETER: In anticipation, Robin had already set in motion a feasibility study regarding return to the islands and we then speeded it up. However, on closer examination, none of this seemed such a great idea – the feasibility study came back with a number of hefty question marks.

COUNS: I heard there were two drafts of the feasibility study, and they conveniently ignored the first one.

PETER: I say, Professor, is your wife a bit of a conspiracy theorist…

CONSERV: Sorry/ Mary.

COUNS: I'm sorry, it's fascinating/ to hear the official version.

CONSERV: Shouldn't you go and get the boy?

PETER: Next you will be telling us/ the moon landings were –

COUNS: The moon landings were faked, I know. Sorry, please go on.

PETER: Well I shall attempt to bring us up to date. So after Robin rather rashly saying the islanders could go back to the outer islands.

CONSERV: Presumably that would have been hugely expensive for the State.

PETER: Precisely – and they promptly launched private law proceedings, with a view to getting compensation which might help finance their resettlement plans. This one didn't fly, however.

COUNS: Why not?

PETER: They had been compensated in 1982, and had signed papers which comprehensively accepted that that was it.

COUNS: Most of them couldn't read or write.

CONSERV: Mary –

PETER: *(Reassuring CONSERVATIONIST.)* It's fine – *(To COUNSELLOR.)* they signed papers, /they had advice.

COUNS: Thumbprints/

PETER: The world is a tough place, I am just talking about law here.

COUNS: What about human rights?

PETER: Well, now you have it, I will come to that in a moment – anyway, in 2004 we enacted another Order in Council to prevent the Chagossians returning to any of the islands.

And, finally we come to Bancoult 2, a second case headed by this tenacious electrician and his Chagos Refugee Group – this case essentially questioned whether these orders in council were *ultra vires*.

COUNS: – ?

PETER: Beyond the lawful powers of the sovereign. This is the big one as far as law is concerned, because it challenges the whole validity of primary legislation.

COUNS: This is about the fact that we don't have a written constitution.

PETER: Right, that's right. Anyway, it goes to the Lords and by a majority decision, the Chagossians lost.

COUNS: On what grounds?

PETER: Well, amongst other things, the judge questioned whether their star witness, a very sprightly old lady was telling a few porkies/

COUNS: Madame Talate/

PETER: Could be – anyway, there were some inconsistencies in her testimony, apparently she couldn't possibly have witnessed all the things she claimed to have, she had acquired extra memories.

COUNS: Jesus, don't they get it, she's been telling these stories for years, it's a form of cultural resilience, a survival technique, like a national memory.

PETER: Fiction won't stand up in court I am afraid – So now they have gone to the European Court of Justice to seek redress there, and we await the outcome. Phew – I rather wish I hadn't started that. Where is that wine?

CONSERV: Thanks, very comprehensive.

COUNS: Very comprehensive indeed – so if nothing happens, we and the Yanks can go on using Diego Garcia for bombing and extraordinary rendition flights/

PETER: Not proven/

COUNS: While the poor Chagossians are left out in the cold, in Mauritius and the/ Seychelles

PETER: Actually we have a fairly substantial Chagossian community in Crawley now/,

COUNS: I know/

PETER: Many of whom are very gratefully enjoying the fruits of British citizenship.

COUNS: A few Man Fridays.

PETER: I think you will find it's a few <u>Men</u> Fridays. Civil service very punctilious about syntax in those days.

COUNS: For Christ's sake.

PETER: Mary – nobody is defending any of this. It's politics, world politics. As Tony is so fond of saying, sometimes we have to make tough choices.

COUNS: You say it so blithely, sitting in a posh restaurant in Mayfair.

CONSERV: Mary, I would like you to go now, / please

PETER: Would it make it better if I was saying it in a soup kitchen/ – I really don't see the relevance.

COUNS: OK, right, sorry, yes, I'm going.

PETER: Very nice to meet you.

COUNS: And you. *(To CONSERV.)* I'll give you a ring later.

She goes.

CONSERV: I am terribly sorry, I had no idea she was going to get so/ aeriated.

PETER: It's quite alright.

CONSERV: I had no intention of subjecting you/ to that.

PETER: It's quite alright. *(Beat.)* So, tell me a bit more about your proposal. The MPA.

CONSERV: She has a client/

PETER: It's fine. The MPA.

CONSERV: Well it's fairly straightforward really. Partly because of everything that has happened, law of unintended consequences and all that, the Chagos Islands have the best and most intact reef in the world.

PETER: And you want to make it into a marine park.

CONSERV: Not a park exactly: a Marine Protection Area.

PETER: The difference being?

CONSERV: The difference being that this would be a complete No-Take zone.

PETER: No fishing at all.

CONSERV: No fishing by anyone, be it Sri Lankan illegals, licensed Japanese trawlers, even the Yachties.

PETER: Suppose the Chagossians won the right to return.

CONSERV: *(Beat.)* We don't have a position on that.

PETER: No, I mean, would they be allowed to fish?

CONSERV: Well, we don't necessarily all agree on this one, but frankly, as far as I am concerned, preferably, No.

PETER: No take means no take.

CONSERV: I mean, as I understand it, one of the Chagossian proposals is to stimulate a tourist industry, like in the Seychelles and Mauritius, but that would be an absolute disaster.

PETER: Why?

CONSERV: Look what happened, there, look at the state of their reefs.

PETER: The Chagos is better?

CONSERV: Ten million times better. And more resilient. After El Niño caused a massive bleaching event all round the world, the Chagos has recovered incredibly quickly. Quite quite wonderful.

PETER: What I can say is that David and Tony are broadly very receptive to this idea/

CONSERV: Great.

PETER: It has the dual advantage of making a return less probable/

CONSERV: That's not our declared intention –

PETER: Of course, but it does – how could they possibly return if the whole area is a Marine Park – and it can be shrouded in a lovely touchy feely green motivation.

CONSERV: Friends of the Earth and Greenpeace are already backing it. And this Swiss businessman may put up the money.

PETER: Green and cheap – woohoo. So what I am telling you is, the ground is fertile. I assume you are not too bothered by the presence of the base?

CONSERV: We recognise that that is a given.

PETER: Precisely – so it's win-win all round.

CONSERV: Good.

PETER: Yes. Good. Good good good. Shall we? Where's our food?

SCENE 26

The Wreck of the Diego.

DUSSERCLE: On the good ship Diego, we are stuck on the reef off Ile Danger in June 1935. One man is pushing out a boat, a pirogue. Salvation, salvation. If only he can reach us if only he can reach us. Que dieu lui vienne en aide. It is Arthur Talate, Father of Lisette Talate, born on Trois Frère like two generations of Talate before him. I Roger Dussercle, Priest of the Catholic Church, give thanks to Talate and to God.

So near and yet so far – Talate struggles with his paddle, trying to cross the breakers which foam with rage. The waves, thirty foot high, completely drench him, filling the pirogue, tipping it over, sometimes throwing it brutally onto the reefs. Talate is not discouraged. Twenty times Talate renews his efforts, perilous in so many ways – the sea, the tide, the reefs, the darkness and the sharks – and twenty times the sea casts him back to land. We are at its mercy in the waves, like a toy in the hands of an angry child.

Till finally the brave Talate breaks through the waves with a rope held in his teeth, and once we are connected to Arthur Talate, we are all saved.

SCENE 27

Sainsbury's, Mile End Road, London, May 2010

CONSERV: So now we need bloody dogfood – how on earth did I let myself be persuaded, it's against all my principles/

COUNS: Come on, Bruno loves him.

CONSERV: Breeding animals for pets.

COUNS: Ronnie Barker is a rescue dog for Christ's sake – he would have just quietly died in Battersea if we hadn't got him.

CONSERV: You do realise all the shit that goes into dogfood I presume?

COUNS: I think it's on the last aisle.

He is gone. PROSPER enters, edgy.

PROSPER: Hey. Mary?

COUNS: Prosper. How are you?

PROSPER: I am good, I am good, how are you? How's your baby?

COUNS: Bruno.

PROSPER: Bruno.

COUNS: Not such a baby, he's four now.

PROSPER: Mary has a little lamb.

COUNS: How is your life? It's nice to see you.

PROSPER: Fine, The Queen asked me to be Prime Minister, now I am running the country.

COUNS: Right.

PROSPER: Just kidding.

COUNS: Oh.

PROSPER: You disappeared.

COUNS: Did I? I don't know who disappeared first. There were rather long gaps between your visits.

PROSPER: I went to the centre, they told me I couldn't see you anymore.

COUNS: I decided to stop work, at least for a year or two.

PROSPER: I used to enjoy our chats.

COUNS: Did you? I am sure you could see someone else.

PROSPER: I am still on the journey.

COUNS: We're all on a journey.

PROSPER: But I am almost there.

COUNS: Really.

PROSPER: I almost have the whole map, how it's all connected.

COUNS: And what will you do, when you have made all the connections?

PROSPER: Something. Something needs to be done.

COUNS: Really? Isn't it more important just to get on with life?

PROSPER: Imagine if all my ancestors rose up out of their graves on Diego Garcia, and connected with all the other outcasts, all the homeless people and refugees and all the other 'ti-dimoun' in the world, imagine what an army that would be…

COUNS: Quite something.

PROSPER: It would be a force to be reckoned with.

Pause.

COUNS: Well, nice to see you again.

PROSPER: You too. *(He starts going.)*

COUNS: Prosper…?

PROSPER: Yeah?

Beat.

COUNS: Nothing.

She moves off, joined by CONSERVATIONIST husband with trolley, PROSPER notices the connection.

CONSERV: *(Exiting.)* I bought Ronnie one of these balls, they were on special offer.

SCENE 28

PROSPER's dream where he makes connections.

In this dream, which will involve much animation, many past faces come together and connect up, like the reef building process. This includes all the players in the Strategic Island Concept, MRS TALATE, the films of donkeys and children, and finally the presence of the CONSERVATIONIST and his relationship to the COUNSELLOR. This is played out on screen, while key members of the company, including the COUNSELLOR, sing 'Dem Bones'.

A group of skeleton costumed people, rise from their graves to the tune of 'Dem Bones'. Prosper piles things up, aniwawa-style.

SCENE 29

July 2010.

A white man, the CONSERVATIONIST, is mounting a podium to speak to a Seminar, he is being applauded, maybe there are images of reef. There are members of the company in the audience, some of whom will descend at the end, to congratulate him; others will stay in audience, laptops open.

CONSERV: Thank you Minister, thank you all. I want to end on the positive note this deserves.

We did it. The dream has come true. Yeah! And it's a victory we can all savour.

I know you don't need persuading – but I wanted to share with you my personal passion, the driver that has kept me going. Some of you know that my first completed work was on the manta ray – I was first to realise that the giant manta was in fact a different species. *(Woop from audience.)*

Thanks – *(Peering.)* – Colin?

VOICE: Duncan, actually.

Laughter.

CONSERV: Sorry Duncan, you know my problem.

More laughter.

When I first found the giant manta, this noble creature had nowhere to run. Like an aeroplane running out of fuel – and those of you who have seen it know that it is a bit like a small aeroplane, up to seven metres from wing to wing, sleek, black, double hulled, beautiful – like an aeroplane without a runway to land on, cruising up to five hundred miles in its search. Through no fault of his own, this fine fellow finds himself the quarry of vast fleets of Chinese trawlers, engaged in their endless national quest for its body parts for that oh-so unscientific of obsessions known as Chinese medicine.

Now my old friend has somewhere to run, somewhere to hide, safely, along with a plethora of other wonders of nature. The waters around the Chagos Islands are astonishingly rich: 220 coral species, 1,000 species of fish, the breeding grounds for 17 kinds of seabird, 700 hawksbill and 800 green turtles – and let's not forget the world's largest land arthropod, the coconut crab, for whom these pristine islands are home.

CONSERV: And yes, they are now almost completely free of human interference – apart from the occasional visiting yachties and the odd GI of course. It is paradise over there, and it must not become paradise lost. And now, thanks to all our efforts, and thanks to the enlightened intervention of this government, with the creation of a full No-Take Marine Protection Area, it won't be. Thank you.

Applause. Various attendees cluster round him, shake hands etc., at least one he takes a photograph of, then they leave. He is dealing with his slides etc., a black man is hovering, he has a Sainsbury's bag with things in it.

PROSPER: Hi.

CONSERV: Hello.

PROSPER: You don't remember me?

CONSERV: Erm…

PROSPER: The seminar last year –

CONSERV: I do a lot of seminars – jog my memory.

PROSPER: You were speaking about the reefs and their resilience, their recovery from El Niño, you were very passionate.

CONSERV: Right – sorry, do you work for one of the biology faculties?

PROSPER: I am unemployed.

CONSERV: Sorry to hear that. *(Beat.)* I have a defect, a face recognition defect, its latin name is prosopagnosia, more commonly, face-blindness, I don't recognise people, sometimes I take photos.

PROSPER: Like a spy.

CONSERV: Like I want to remember people. *(Beat.)* Most people have a kind of rolodex of faces in their head, to recognise others, to work out who is a significant other and who is just an other. I have to take photos.

PROSPER: You never took a photograph of me.

CONSERV: OK… You are a Chagossian.

PROSPER: Bingo.

CONSERV: You don't sound it.

PROSPER: So you got what you wanted. A safe haven for the fishes.

CONSERV: The MPA will be good for all species – Fishes, turtles, birds.

PROSPER: The boobies and hawksbills.

CONSERV: You know your stuff.

PROSPER: I read up on it. And it's my culture.

CONSERV: OK. *(Pause.)* Well, I must be getting on. Nice to meet you…?

PROSPER: Prosper.

CONSERV: Nice to meet you Prosper.

PROSPER: *(Bars the way.)* I haven't finished.

Pause.

CONSERV: Look you seem to be angry with me – I don't know why/ – we don't even know each other.

PROSPER: I am not a significant other./ Just an other.

CONSERV: If it's about what happened to your people, I really sympathise, it's terrible, but I am nothing to do with that. I am just a humble conservationist trying to preserve what little nature's left in the world.

PROSPER: And it's better without us/

CONSERV: I don't have a position on that. We have had Chagossians at all the meetings, sometimes they have spoken.

PROSPER: It's better without us now, as it was better without us before. For you a turtle matters more than a person.

CONSERV: That's not what I said, and not what I think.

The CONSERVATIONIST's mobile starts to ring.

Of course you are more important than a turtle.

PROSPER: Thank you.

CONSERVATIONIST struggles to get phone out, looks at caller display.

CONSERV: That's not the choice. Excuse me, I have to take this call.

Hey, hey, hey, slow down, start again – what happened?

OK. So when exactly did Ronnie Barker go missing?

PROSPER is playing with images on CONSERVATIONIST's laptop – pictures of people.

Why does he have to be dead – He'll come back. Trust me. At his age, he knows what he is doing. He's probably got a girlfriend.

Look I can't talk right now, *(To PROSPER.)* would you leave that alone please?

I'm dealing with something, talk to Mum, I'll call back in a bit.

PROSPER: *(Referring to the projected images.)* Who're all the people?

CONSERV: Friends, acquaintances, I told you I suffer from face-blindness, it's none of your business.

(Referring to image on screen and trying to get laptop back.) – that's my son, I was just speaking to him, do you mind...?

PROSPER: You need a photo to remember what your son looks like?

CONSERV: Of course not, that's my screen-saver

PROSPER gives laptop back.

Beat.

Look – the Chagos Islands happen to be pristine, because of that terrible thing that happened forty years ago.

PROSPER: You all let it happen.

CONSERV: I wasn't involved. I was hardly even born then. The past is another country my friend.

PROSPER: I am not your friend. If I was your friend, you would have made as much effort campaigning for me and my people as you made to protect your precious boobies.

CONSERV: It's the reef, not the boobies. Prosper, I can see you are really really angry. And I am really really sorry. But we can't all fight every battle, however much we might want to.

PROSPER: My people fought a battle.

CONSERV: I know – very bravely too, right up through the courts. But I am nothing to do with that.

PROSPER: You choose not to be.

CONSERV: OK. I choose. So can I go now, please?

PROSPER: I thought you wanted to end on a positive note –

CONSERV: I do.

PROSPER: So before you end, because perhaps you are right, perhaps it is time to end – wait a little moment and listen? Do you hear? *(There is nothing.)*

CONSERV: What?

Hear what?

We hear a bell, CONSERVATIONIST doesn't.

PROSPER: That's what you call a wake-up call. We call it the bellcall.

CONSERV: I don't know what…/ I am supposed to be listening to.

PROSPER: Listen to the voices. See if they have faces in your rolodex…

Pause.

CONSERV: I am sorry, we are not hearing the same things.

PROSPER: You're deaf.

CONSERV: Maybe.

PROSPER: Deaf and blind. You cannot distinguish between people. You have only your family that you recognise, and no one else exists. And you think that gives you the right to make the world as you want it.

CONSERV: I really don't/ think that's fair –

PROSPER: Your wife sees more than you do.

Beat.

CONSERV: I beg your pardon?

PROSPER: She's wiser than you.

CONSERV: What has my wife/ got to do?

PROSPER: But in the end she dropped it too.

CONSERV: Right –

PROSPER: She didn't want to get involved.

CONSERV: I begin to get this.

PROSPER: Making connections…?

CONSERV: Erm –

PROSPER: Come on, spit it out.

CONSERV: What?

PROSPER: You know who I am.

CONSERV: You are –

PROSPER: I have become a significant other.

CONSERV: You are –

PROSPER: I know Ronnie Barker too.

CONSERV: Have you been stalking me? This is some kind of plot.

PROSPER: Plot? That's just your fantasy – there's no plot.

CONSERV: Ronnie Barker –

PROSPER: He's lovely.

COUNSELLOR comes in, not immediately noticing PROSPER.

COUNS: Teddy, I can't stay for the drinks, Bruno is distraught about the dog.

PROSPER: Ronnie Barker's gone missing.

COUNS: *(Sees him.)* Prosper.

CONSERV: Prosper seems to know us very well.

PROSPER: Hi Mary.

COUNS: How are you?

PROSPER: I am fine. You know Professor Hibbert I think?

COUNS: It's just coincidence Prosper –

PROSPER: Coincidence or conspiracy?

CONSERV: Coincidence, really/

COUNS: Teddy please.

PROSPER: What does it take to get noticed in this world? You have to do something –

COUNS: Let's sit down and talk this out.

PROSPER: You have to do something big, something that affects the big world –

CONSERV: Prosper, we are not even part of the Big World.

COUNS: Teddy –

PROSPER: Like if you killed the Queen's corgis – now that would make them sit up, that would make the news.

CONSERV: Have you done something to Ronnie Barker?

PROSPER: Would that hurt? If I did something to Ronnie Barker, would that hurt?

COUNS: It would hurt our son/ –

CONSERV: It would hurt me actually.

PROSPER: Bruno/

CONSERV: Jesus, you are going to hurt/ a harmless animal.

COUNS: But he would get over it. In time.

CONSERV: Mary, what on earth/

COUNS: As you will. In time.

PROSPER: What does it all add up to? I've found out so much, I have made all the connections, I understand everything – and it just makes it worse.

COUNS: Why is it worse?

PROSPER: Because there is nothing we can do – Robinson Crusoe will tolerate Man Friday as his faithful servant, but if Man Friday says he wants a piece of the action…let's get outta here, this island's ours.

COUNS: Prosper – there's nothing I can say. You are right.

CONSERV: Hold on –

COUNS: But if you do anything silly, they will just lock you up. Think about all the other little people, all the other ti dimoun. What will happen to them?

Pause.

PROSPER: I have to go. What do you think the dog represents, Mary?

COUNS: *(Beat.)* A dog. It represents a dog.

PROSPER: Who knows. Every dog has its day. Nice to see you, Mary.

He leaves.

CONSERV: Jesus –

COUNS: Don't say anything.

CONSERV: Where's Bruno.

COUNS: He's with the au pair. Don't say anything.

CONSERV: – we should call the police.

COUNS: I thought you didn't want to get involved. Why start now –

CONSERV: Are you completely loopy too? The man's a fucking psycho.

Dog ball bounces on from offstage.

COUNS: Hey – Ronnie.

CONSERV: There you are.

COUNS: I knew he wouldn't hurt him.

CONSERV: Nutter. Complete nutter.

COUNS: Stop it. Let's go home. We are able to go home. Bruno will be waiting.

CONSERV: Bloody nightmare.

SCENE 30

COUNSELLOR's room.

PROSPER breaks into the COUNSELLOR's office, he looks into the fishtank. COUNSELLOR is ghostly present, reading the letter. PROSPER has his bag, machete, Bible, Shakespeare in it. Sits, reads.

COUNS: So then Claudette came along.

We were living near Port Louis at the time. Brian was making music, Sega mixed with reggae, seggae they called it, I was along for the ride. And after those boats came in 1972/73, there were all these poor souls looking for work. The Chagossian men didn't know anything other than coconuts, and there were so many Mauritians out of work at that time, they got priority. A lucky few got work in the docks, most just wandered around lost. And the women were the same, they'd look for work as maids or go on the game, a lot moved into prostitution.

Storm brews up.

And one day in 1979, along came Claudette – Cyclone Claudette, she was a big one – and the morning after when a girl came to our door, everything was still a mess, trees down all over, all their shacks were completely flattened, and the wind is still howling and swirling *(We see the following and hear it.)* – this girl comes to the door, asks if we have any work for her, she has this beautiful boy hanging onto her legs, looking out at the world through her legs. She's speaking patois and neither of us understood a word she was saying. Sagren she kept saying, sagren, that means sadness, I know now. She was out of it, her eyes were bloodshot, and though we couldn't understand we understood when she said she would do anything, and she meant it. And I saw that boy, and I wanted him and immediately I told her I would give her money and take the boy off her hands. And the woman cried, because she knew she was going to say yes, she cried till she had no tears left, and then she handed you over, and you didn't know what was happening, but you knew it wasn't good, and you shouted for her, but she was gone, and you were in our care. And that's all I know. I am sure she was a fine woman and I am sure she didn't give you up lightly. You're a child of the storm, a child of Claudette. Have a great life. Prosper.

The woman you called your mother.

PROSPER: … And our little life is rounded with a sleep.

He puts his face into the water. His image appears on screen. The lighthouse flash dazzles the audience. We lose him on stage, but he dives into the fishtank on screen. He finds himself swimming on the reef. Huge image of pristine reef on screen. Airswimmers may appear. If possible a manta ray swims out over the audience. Blackout.

The End.

ALSO FROM CARDBOARD CITIZENS

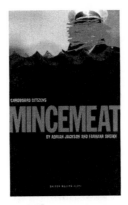

Mincemeat
by Adrian Jackson, Farhana Sheikh

'You know that feeling when you wake up and you don't know where you are, you don't know what you've done, you're not sure if you might have committed some awful crime…and sometimes it stays with you all morning…'

A narrative that crosses time and territory to find answers to questions of identity and matters of life and death, *Mincemeat* unravels the truths and the untruths surrounding a World War Two intelligence operation.

First performed in June 2001, *Mincemeat* features testimony, speculation and outright lies: don't miss the shocking truth behind an event that changed history.

£9.99 / 9781840029352

WWW.OBERONBOOKS.COM